THE BLACK PERSON'S GUIDES

THE COLORS OF LOVE

The Black Person's Guide to Interracial Relationships

KIMBERLY HOHMAN

Lawrence Hill Books

Library of Congress Cataloging-in-Publication Data

Hohman, Kimberly
The colors of love : the black person's guide to interracial relationships /
    Kimberly Hohman.—1st ed.
p. cm.
Includes bibliographical references.
ISBN 1-55652-467-6
1. Interracial dating—United States. 2. Interracial marriage—United
    States. 3. Couples—United States—Interviews. I. Title.
HQ801.8 .H64 2002
306.73'089'04—dc21

2002004208

*To Pap Spack, whose courage and commitment to his family
gave me all the reasons I needed to write this book.
And to Brian, whose unbounded support and belief in me
is matched only by his dedication and love.*

Cover and interior design: Monica Baziuk
Cover photograph: Francesca Yorke/Getty Images

©2002 Kimberly Hohman
First edition
Published by Lawrence Hill Books
An imprint of Chicago Review Press, Incorporated
814 North Franklin Street
Chicago, Illinois 60610
ISBN 1-55652-467-6
Printed in the United States of America
5 4 3 2 1

CONTENTS

✧

Conclusion 173

Resources 175

Notes 192

ACKNOWLEDGMENTS

FIRST AND FOREMOST, many, many thanks to all the couples who so willingly agreed to share their stories within these pages. You've all given me (and the readers) a glimpse into the beauty—and normalcy—that can come when we love without fear. You've confirmed what we always knew to be true. To the interracial community across the Web (and the world) that is so generous, welcoming, and willing to help. To Yuval for giving me the opportunity to fulfill a dream and helping me to make it better than I thought possible. To my kids for putting up with many more "in a minutes" during the writing of this book than any four- and five-year-old should be expected to endure, and for doing it without complaint. To Brian for allowing me to lean and vent and cry and celebrate and for always keeping up with the conversation no matter how many times I change the subject. And to the Spacks and the Ways and my entire extended family for being models of the kinds of families all interracial couples should be so lucky to be surrounded by—for your tolerance, your kindness, your support, and your love.

INTRODUCTION

INTERRACIAL RELATIONSHIPS ARE nothing new. Blacks and whites in the United States have been falling in love since the days of slavery, but over the years interracial couples have learned the hard way that falling in love and making a life together don't always go hand in hand.

In 1958, Mildred Jeter and Richard Loving were forced to leave their Virginia home and travel to Washington, D.C., in order to wed. Upon returning to Virginia to begin their life together, the couple was charged with violating the state's anti-miscegenation laws. They pled guilty and were each sentenced to one year in prison. The trial judge suspended the sentence on the condition that the couple leave their home state, promising not to return together for twenty-five years.

The Lovings did leave Virginia for Washington, D.C., where they made their home. But rather than take this injustice lying down, they decided to make a mark that would forever change history—the Lovings filed suit against the state of Virginia and, in 1967, won a Supreme Court decision that found bans on interracial marriage to be unconstitutional.

When the Lovings were married, they were flying colorblind into the future in a society that most assuredly was not. In 1958, interracial marriage wasn't just against the law in many states, it was practically unheard of. Family and friends, both black and white, would certainly disapprove of such a union and there were no such things as support groups for interracial couples. But things are getting better.

Since then, interracial marriage has become increasingly common. Between 1960 and 1970 alone, the rate of interracial marriage in the United States increased by nearly 900 percent, and the numbers are continuing to grow. In 1960, according to the U.S. Census Bureau, there were 149,000 married interracial couples. By 2000, that number had increased to over two million. Black/white interracial marriages accounted for nearly 300,000 of the interracial marriages in the United States in 1994. In 1990, nearly 8 percent of all married black men between twenty-four and thirty-five were married to non-blacks. And though black women are only about half as likely to marry interracially as their male counterparts, the interracial marriage rates for sisters are climbing faster than those of the brothers. Along with this growth has come increasing acceptance of mixed-race couples. Families of all races are more willing to accept an in-law of a different race than ever before, and interracial couples are drawing fewer stares and nasty remarks.

But despite increases in frequency and acceptance of interracial relationships, interracial couples still face adversity and issues such as continued disapproval from society and the challenges of raising biracial children. There is still an unfortunate lack of support and information available to blacks who choose to cross the racial divide in pursuit of love. Because interracial couples tend to be fragmented in their social alliances, chances are that in addition to a lack of information, there is also a lack of true peers.

This book will address these issues from a black perspective.

With a dozen years invested in my own interracial relationship and two generations of interracial relationships in my family prior to my own, I've done a lot of thinking and talking about the unique aspects of interracial families. In addition, over the years I've talked to numerous interracial couples about their experiences. From these experiences, I've extracted the threads that are common to blacks in interracial relationships and found that with a little common sense, a little hope, and a lot of love, interracial relationships can and do flourish.

From interracial dating, through marriage and child rearing, I'll write frankly about racism and discrimination, dealing with disapproving relatives, blending cultures and traditions in your home, and celebrating the richness that an interracial relationship will undoubtedly bring to your lives.

Throughout the book, you'll also have the opportunity to meet several interracial couples. I've tried to share these couples' wisdom to help readers build strong unions with their chosen partners.

Each chapter of the book can be read independently of the others, so that you'll be able to rely on it as a handy guide through all the stages of your relationship and as you journey through your own unique experiences.

Today interracial relationships are flourishing like never before and, as those of us involved in them have learned, the strengths of interracial relationships can far outweigh the drawbacks. In fact, there's a good chance that as your travel the road of life together you'll start to notice that mixed-race relationships even offer some advantages over same-race relationships. No wonder there's an evolution going on! Interracial relationships have long been an earmark for the state of race relations. If the current growth and success rates of interracial relationships are any indication, the future looks mighty bright.

PART I

IN THE BEGINNING

MEETING YOUR MATCH

IF YOU'RE CONSIDERING dating interracially for the first time, you're probably anxious, excited, and maybe even afraid. Interracial relationships shouldn't be scary—at least no scarier than any other relationship. Unfortunately, though, interracial couples still face many obstacles that same-race couples don't, such as disapproving families, society's naysayers, and, less commonly, out-and-out victimization. Deciding to date interracially—and I use the term *deciding* for lack of a better word—means consciously accepting these obstacles. It means saying, "I am willing to forego the luxuries afforded to same-race couples in favor of the potential of being ostracized by my family and friends, as well as almost certain disapproval from some total strangers." Sound menacing? It may very well be. On the other hand, deciding to date interracially isn't generally a conscious decision.

The cliché goes: You don't choose who you love. The reality is: Most people are hit with an interracial attraction well before they've had a chance to think about whether or not it's something they'd actively put in their game plan. If you're reading this book, you've probably already found yourself attracted to someone of another race. Instead of asking yourself "Do I think that white guy is hot?" you're likely thinking more along the lines of "Am I prepared to enter into a relationship that will set me apart from my peers and make me something of a spectacle in society?" And that's a wise way to be thinking, because being prepared for an interracial relationship can help you avoid a lot of drama and unnecessary surprises.

There won't always be definitive answers to the questions you'll have about interracial dating, but by learning from the experiences of those who have been there, you will start to gain insight that you can apply to your own relationship. In my research and discussions with interracial couples, I've found there are several common questions that people in the early stages of interracial dating frequently ask.

FREQUENTLY ASKED QUESTIONS

Is It Wrong to Be Solely Attracted to People of Another Race?

The debate about this question is probably as old as interracial relationships themselves. To my knowledge, no one has yet come up with a definitive answer, but my personal thinking on it goes something like this: If you could get people to answer honestly, most would tell you that physical attraction is the first thing they appreciate about a potential mate. Various studies generally confirm this notion and, in fact, physical appearance is the top priority of respondents in many polls. If you ask me, there's no shame in that game; it certainly can't hurt to be physically attracted to your mate. Just as some folks prefer dark hair or a tall build, some have skin color preferences that make them gravitate to certain people more than others. On that level, interracial dating is no more controversial than a blond person being attracted to and dating a redhead. The trouble is that in our society skin color equals race, and race obviously carries with it a much more complicated history than hair color. But that in and of itself isn't the whole problem. The problem is people who are after something more than a simple physical attraction to another race.

You know the type and you know they're out there—people who seek out interracial relationships just to spite someone (usually a parent they know will disapprove), or people who date outside of their race just because their peers are doing it. In these relationships, one partner usually ends up becoming a pawn in the game, where it's not about *who* they are, but *what color* they are.

How Do I Know When It's "Jungle Fever"?

"He's got jungle fever. She's got jungle fever." Sing it with me.

I have to admit that for the longest time, I didn't understand "jungle fever." I always assumed it was simply a term used to describe an interracial couple, and I used it jokingly with friends. One day, I was talking to a black girlfriend of mine who was lamenting about the guy she was dating—who just happened to be white. Things were going well in the relationship, but for some reason she still had some niggling doubts about his intentions. She just couldn't shake his repeated comments about her exotic looks, and the fact that he made a random remark about black women being wild in bed had her feeling, well, a little scared.

The true meaning of *jungle fever* finally clicked for me that day. *Jungle fever* is when your mate is interested solely in your race and not in the true you. It's the white guy who just wants to experiment with a dark beauty or the white girl who is determined to find out if size really does matter. True, you want a mate who is captivated by you, but not for all the wrong reasons. If your new partner constantly mentions those age-old myths about phallic size, rumors about bedroom behavior, or exoticness, run fast and far.

On the flip side, there are also brothers and sisters who date people of other races for all the wrong reasons. You already know the reasons, because they spark debates like, "You're only dating that white person because you're a self-hating African American." All of the reasons run along that same vein:

"You hate your own race."

"You're trying to be better than the rest of us."

"You want light-skinned babies."

These accusations are ugly, but even uglier is the possibility that there are black folks dating white people for exactly those reasons. If you're among them, I recommend putting this book down and giving some real thought to why you're considering interracial dating. Love and relationships should be about mutual respect and admiration for your partner. If you're in a relationship for some of the previously mentioned reasons, there's a good chance you lack self-respect. Without that, what can you possibly offer your partner?

Is It Really That Hard to Date Interracially?

As with any type of relationship, individual experiences vary widely; from the couple who's seen nothing but hate and discontent in the wake of their relationship, to the couple who has never had so much as an eyelash batted in their direction as a result of their relationship. My experience has been that while there are couples on both ends of that spectrum, the vast majority of couples' realities lie somewhere between wanting to live a friction-free life and realizing that the world is an imperfect place.

Whether or not your interracial experience is a difficult one depends heavily on several factors (all of which will be discussed in greater depth later on in the book): both your and your partner's family and friends' acceptance of interracial relationships, your level of comfort with being seen by society as something of a novelty, your geographical location, your commitment to your relationship, and both your and your partner's self-confidence.

While a relationship can survive the misfortune of having negative marks in all of the above categories, having any or all of those things in your favor will make an interracial relationship much easier. Assessing each factor will help you determine, to some extent, whether the road ahead will be a rough one.

Many interracial couples find that the stress of these challenges can be diminished by accepting that some things will be harder for them than they are for same-race couples. There's no doubt that interracial couples face hurdles and that, when you add them to the hurdles that face any couple, they can seem overwhelming. But if you find your true love in a person of another race and you're committed to that love, any hurdle can be overcome.

Will I Experience More Disapproval from Within My Racial Group or from Outside?

Those in interracial relationships can expect disapproval from others. Disapproval from your family is probably the most hurtful because it feels like being rejected by the people you care about most. When the disapproval comes from strangers, you're much more likely to offer up a relevant hand gesture and get on with your business. But when the disapproval comes from peers of your racial group who might or might not know you well, you're more likely to start to doubt your decisions, your choices, and your situation. The disapproval of your peers can make you re-examine whether your relationship is really OK, because you rarely think of your peers as old-fashioned or having antiquated ideas about race, which you'd be more likely to assume of your family.

While peer pressure is commonly thought of as an adolescent problem, it can continue to affect us as adults. Wanting to be accepted by those we consider our equals has as much to do with simple human nature as it does with a desire to boost self-confidence. But peer pressure can be a good thing if it strengthens your convictions. Also, confrontation by your peers gives you an opportunity to educate those who disapprove and possibly cause them to rethink their attitudes.

While societal reactions to interracial relationships will be discussed at greater length later in the book, whether you experience more disapproval from within or from outside your race group tends to depend on the race group of which you're a member. Whites in interracial relationships tend to experience more condemnation from other whites, but because it's more expected, it may be somewhat easier to deal with. Black people are usually less likely to face disapproving attitudes from other blacks, but may find the disapproval they do face harder to swallow because it comes as more of a shock. One study[1] of 100 black/white interracial relationships conducted by Dr. Sheryline A. Zebroski between 1989 and 1991 found that people in such relationships were more likely to rate people of the same race and sex as most supportive of their relationship. They were also more likely to rate people of the opposite sex but same race as most opposed to their relationship.

You might find these statistics useful as you attempt to gauge your own expectations.

RESOURCES AND IDEAS FOR MEETING AND APPROACHING PEOPLE OF OTHER RACES

If you're not already in a relationship but you'd like to be, you're probably looking for someone intelligent, fascinating, attractive, and ambitious—but so is every other single person in the world. What's a person to do? From what I hear talking to single friends, today's singles scene isn't always fun. The challenge of the desire to date interracially is that, since not everyone has given it the consideration you have, you may find it difficult to hook up with someone of another race. Antiquated as it sounds, there's no easy way to tell if someone is down with interracial dating, so you may be looking rejection in the face if you're considering asking out a stranger in a bar, especially if he or she has never dated interracially. Worse, unless he or she is sporting a pointed hat and a white sheet, it's hard to tell a racist by looks. You certainly don't want to set yourself up for an encounter with any outwardly attractive but inwardly ugly person.

Personally, I prefer the just-let-it-happen approach to meeting the love of your life. Many interracial couples have found love in the most common ways: through their jobs, via a shared interest, or from a casual friendship that developed into something more. Indeed, the majority of the couples I spoke with in the preparation for this book explained that they were friends for some time before they became a couple. According to Dr. Zebroski's study, interracial couples were:

- more likely to have met through their jobs than in school, in their neighborhoods, in church, or through recreational activities
- more likely to admit that their courtship began through repeated casual conversations rather than with immediate physical attraction, friendship over a period of time, or after a close association (e.g., work relationship, casual friendship) with each other

- more likely to admit that their initial attraction to each other was their shared interests as compared with shared beliefs, physical attraction, or because their partner held an important position in a group

But if that road has thus far proved to be a dead end for you, maybe you're ready to start looking down other avenues. If you're still waiting to exhale or are looking to get your groove back, here are some resources for breaking down the barriers to the interracial dating world.

Interracial/Multicultural Clubs

Many bigger cities and even some smaller ones with large multicultural populations are launching interracial or multicultural clubs to help like-minded individuals socialize. Clubs like New York City's Swirl Inc. (www.swirlinc.org) provide a social outlet for interracial couples and multiracial people who are interested in seeking out others with similar interests. Organized social events are a wonderful way to meet people and provide networking opportunities unlike those you might be able to develop by going solo.

Diversity Hot Spots

Depending on your geographical location, you may find that heading downtown for your nights out offers you a more diverse crowd to mingle with than hanging out in the more homogeneous suburbs. College and university towns also tend to offer a more racially diverse environment, along with cutting edge nightlife and cultural experiences. Make an effort to seek out ethnically diverse happenings in your town, such as festivals and performances, to see who you might meet.

Internet Dating

Singles around the globe are turning to the Internet as the new singles bar. It's rapidly become recognized as a great resource for meeting like-minded individuals. Because of the successes of Internet match-ups, interracial-friendly dating sites such as InterracialSingles.com (www.

interracialsingles.com) are cropping up across the Web. If you think about it, Internet dating and interracial relationships are a match made in heaven. Where else can you find such large, concentrated groups of single people looking to date interracially? It takes the guesswork out of interracial dating by eliminating the question "But would he/she be up for an interracial relationship?" Of course, the Internet dating scene does have its drawbacks, namely the already discussed and reviled "jungle fever." Plus, finding a reputable dating service can be a challenge. Try doing a search for "interracial" on a search engine and you'll turn up X-rated interracial porn sites. Still, many people in all kinds of relationships swear by the success they've had meeting mates on-line. However, there are a few universal ground rules to observe when hitting the Internet dating scene.

You Lie, You Lie

Don't believe the hype. Recognize that not everything that on-line people tell you is the truth. People lie on-line for one simple reason: it's easy to get away with. Weighing in at 350 pounds and wishing you were thin? Tell him you're a cool 175; he can't see you. Working at the local 7-Eleven and wishing it wasn't so? Tell her you're the CEO of an Internet start-up; she'll never know the difference. According to WiredPatrol (www.WiredPatrol.org), "Women tend to lie about their weight or age, while men tend to lie about their income, level of baldness, and athletic condition." Use good judgment and your best private detective skills to decipher what's fact and what's fiction. On the flip side, it's always a good practice to be honest about yourself when corresponding on-line. No sense telling someone you look "just like Denzel" when you know you don't. If there's a chance you'll end up pursuing the relationship beyond e-mail and on-line chatting, you'll only end getting caught in the end, so don't set yourself up for failure.

Don't Give Up the Digits

Don't reveal personal information on-line—including your last name. There's no need for anyone you meet on-line to know anything more about you than your chat nickname or your (preferably anonymous) e-mail address. Don't tell them where you work, where you live, or any other easily identifiable information. Before you start scoping out the Internet dating scene, take a moment to sign up for a Web-based e-mail address at a site like Yahoo! (www.yahoo.com) or Hotmail (www. hotmail.com). Using this type of e-mail address rather than your personal ISP account provides you with an easy exit in the event that Mr. or Ms. Perfect suddenly turns out to be Mr. or Ms. Fatal Attraction with stalking or bunny-boiling tendencies.

Let it Flow

Take things slowly when you're getting to know someone on-line. One of the greatest benefits of meeting someone on-line is having the chance to get to know them without all the bumbling and fumbling that often comes with the first face-to-face meeting. While on-line dating eliminates the luxury of assessing a person's true physical presence (a picture sent via e-mail might paint a thousand words, but it can't warn you about simple chronic halitosis or flat-out funky B.O.), it does give you the benefit of finding out whether or not a potential suitor can spell and just how well he or she can communicate. Take advantage of an extended on-line courtship period before you make a move to meet in person. The extra time will give you an opportunity to catch any discrepancies in the information your correspondent is feeding you. As the WiredPatrol put it, "Everyone can put their best cyber-foot forward in the first couple of e-mails. Being consistent is tougher. Make sure you keep the old e-mails to compare the information they give you."

Ring My Bell

When you do decide to take the next step in the relationship, make it a phone call rather than a face-to-face meeting. Rather than offering up your home number right off the bat, make arrangements to call your potential date from a pay phone, or give him or her the number of a pay phone near you and arrange a time for the call. It might seem like too much trouble, but keep your personal safety your number-one priority.

If he's serious about you and interested, he'll be taking the same precautions and will understand your desire to protect yourself.

Public Displays

When you do feel comfortable enough to meet in person, choose a very public, well-used, and well-lit location. Bring one of your friends along to cover your back in case of an emergency (not-your-type atrocities or otherwise); if your friend doesn't intend to stay with you for the entire date, make sure he or she has a copy of your itinerary for the day. Arrange for the entire date to take place in public and resist the urge to go home with your date on the very first meeting. If all goes well, there will be plenty of time for that in the future!

If you're smart and cautious, interracial dating on-line needn't be any more dangerous than the bar scene. You might find it the perfect place to meet the love of your life.

❖ Alana and Ty's Story

To say that Alana and Ty fell in love at first sight might be a little misleading. But to them, the experience was nothing less than that.

Neither of them was really looking for love. Alana was a single working mother facing the challenges of raising her young son alone. A former model, Alana wasn't at a loss for dates, but on a whim she decided to place an Internet ad in the AOL personals. Alana thought it might be fun to run her own ad, just to see what kind of response she would get. She never expected to meet her future husband.

Ty was a student who was in the market for love. Browsing through the AOL personals one day, he came across Alana's just-for-fun ad, complete with photo, and immediately knew he was looking at "the one." In his words, Alana had "the most amazing and precious eyes I have ever witnessed." He immediately sent Alana a heartfelt e-mail to share his feelings with her. For Alana, reading Ty's initial e-mail was "when she first glimpsed upon [his] soul."

Thanks to technology, the two, who seemed so destined to be together, were able to connect from three hundred miles apart.

While Alana had previous experiences in interracial relationships (her son is biracial and she has dated men of all races—"anyone who had a great personality and showed an interest in getting to know me as I did them"), this was to be Ty's first interracial romance. "And last," according to Alana, who is determined to see to that! Yet, he wasn't necessarily in the market to date a black woman as he browsed through the personal ads on AOL. He simply found Alana to be "a vision of perfect beauty." Race, he says, was inconsequential.

The two exchanged e-mails for only three days before deciding to meet in person. While that may seem hasty, the couple had spent time on the phone getting to know one another and felt comfortable enough to move on to the next step quickly. Neither of them felt the least bit reluctant to move forward with the meeting.

The couple decided to meet in a public park, where Ty anxiously awaited Alana's arrival with a single red rose. He was immediately taken by Alana and pleased to find that the inner beauty he had come to know via e-mail and on the telephone was equally matched by her physical beauty in person. "A true miracle of God," he recalls thinking on their first face-to-face meeting.

To his dismay, Ty later learned that Alana's first impression was something slightly less ethereal.

"He looks short," Alana remembers thinking.

At 6′3″, one could hardly call Ty "short," but model-tall Alana at 5′11″, not including heels, was looking him straight in the eye.

Any height reservations quickly melted away as the two spent the entire day getting to know one another better.

Since then, life has been good for the newly formed family. Alana and Ty moved to be nearer to each other within two months of that first meeting. They recently became engaged and are busily planning their wedding. Ty currently attends North Carolina State University, Alana's alma mater, where he is majoring in mechanical engineering, coincidentally the same discipline she studied. The two are also applying to attend law school together when Ty completes his undergraduate work. And though there is a somewhat sizable age difference between them, Ty being six years Alana's junior, it hasn't held the two back from relating to one another on an equal level. In fact, they seem to thrive on it.

"I keep her on her feet and light at heart with my youthful enthusiasm," says Ty. "We have the most perfect way of completely complementing each other in every aspect of our lives."

While life is good, the couple has had their share of stumbling blocks on the road to romance. Ty's family initially had some difficulty accepting the relationship.

"They are from a small town and interracial dating is looked down upon," says Alana.

Though the relationship with Ty's family was rocky at first, after much convincing the family finally looked beyond Alana's race and got to know her as a person.

"They finally came around about two months ago and things have been great ever since," she says. "My son calls them Grandma and Grandpa."

Alana's son, Michael, posed another challenge for the family, though it had nothing to do with race and everything to do with the challenges couples face when blending families together.

"My son was jealous of my fiancé because Ty was taking attention away from him."

Since then, Ty and Michael have formed bonds of their own.

"I have come to love him as my own and consider myself so fortunate to have been touched by his life," says Ty.

As for Alana, she can't imagine her life without her soon-to-be husband.

"My fiancé is my best friend, lover, and business partner. He is the most caring and loving person I have ever met. He is great with my son and loves him dearly. I can't imagine life without him. He's the first person I talk to in the morning and the only person I talk to continuously throughout the day through e-mail and phone calls. He is a blessing and I am so grateful to have him."

Despite all the love in the air, the couple remains in touch with reality. Although they see "nothing but each other's heart," they realize that "the world still has a little catching up to do."

Alana's advice for interracial couples? "Go with your heart and don't let others talk you out of being with who you love because of race. The world is changing and becoming more and more accepting of interracial couples. Life is too short to not be with the one you love."

2

MAKING THE COMMITMENT

WHILE YOU MIGHT not consciously decide to fall in love with someone of another race, when it happens, you'll have to make some other decisions. Falling in love is the easy part. Deciding whether or not to pursue an interracial relationship can be more difficult.

If you find yourself in a casual relationship with a person of another race, you might be content to ignore the pressures facing interracial couples in the long term. The early stages of a romance are, after all, about getting to know each other. At that point you're more likely to be focusing on each other than worrying about the people around you. But when you begin to consider the possibility of moving ahead with the relationship (long-term commitment, marriage, kids), you'll be forced to face the issues surrounding interracial relationships today.

The fact is, maintaining a long-term relationship takes a lot of work. Couples of all colors face unavoidable stresses and strains on their relationships. These pressures can test your will to be together, but they can also teach you about yourself and your partner. In an interracial relationship, you're in the unfortunate position of having to face these common struggles while you learn to manage the troubles specific to mixed-race couples. These added burdens make it even more important to communicate well with your partner, especially in the early stages of your relationship. Address the negatives facing your new relationship so that you're both on the same page before you decide to start breaking down doors and burning bridges in your effort to be together.

If your family and friends aren't yet aware of your budding romance, there may be questions about how they'll handle the news. Or you may already know that drama is just around the corner. Even if you're lucky enough to have the full support of your families and friends, issues such as societal discrimination, racism, and raising biracial children deserve your attention as you move forward.

Obviously, the specific issues you face will be unique to your situation, but there are issues common to all who pursue interracial love. Taking cues from the experiences of other couples will help you get a feel for what to expect as you step into a commitment.

LOSING FAMILY AND FRIENDS

In a perfect world, our families and closest friends would accept us unconditionally, for who we are as well as for whom we choose to love. Unfortunately, the world isn't perfect, and neither are those who love us. Losing friends and being shut out by members of your family becomes a very real possibility when you choose to date interracially. Think and talk with your partner about how those close to you will react to your relationship. Target ways of facing any opposing family members (discussed at further length in chapters 5 and 6) and discuss how you'll handle friends, acquaintances, or coworkers who might disapprove of your relationship. Be honest with your mate and realistic about the future of the relationship. If you're going to face the risk of eliminating people from your life because of this relationship, be as sure as possible that your mate is worth the risk.

BEING VIEWED AS DIFFERENT

If you were entering a same-race relationship, you'd give very little thought to what people outside of your circle of two might think. But because interracial relationships remain something of a novelty, yours will be viewed with the same curiosity and, sadly, speculation that faces anything outside of the ordinary. As a result, you and your partner should ready yourselves for stares, whispers, and even wonderment when you enter a room. While this kind of behavior isn't always negative—in fact, you may find that stares are the result of a genuine respect for your ability to foster a relationship in the face of adversity—being the center of attention when you feel you haven't done anything to warrant it, or when you don't particularly want to be, can be uncomfortable. The relationship will suffer if one or both of you isn't prepared to accept unwanted attention, bold questions about your relationship (sometimes from complete strangers), or even—dare I say it—questions about your children's paternity, so it's a good idea to bring these issues to the table before you deepen your commitment.

RACISM AND DISCRIMINATION

Even though attitudes toward interracial relationships are changing, you and your partner may still face racism and discrimination. And though you are already well aware of the discrimination facing people of color in the United States, your partner will be treading new ground in this arena. Warn your new partner that he or she will be up against racist attitudes that are never pretty. Books and literature on the civil rights movement can help your mate begin to understand the issues surrounding race in America. Your mate may never have had the opportunity to fully understand these issues, so don't be surprised or judgmental if he or she hasn't. Also, there are plenty of movies depicting racial issues that can shed light on some of the things African Americans have faced and continue to deal with in the United States. (See the Resources section at the end of this book for a list of suggestions.) Preparing your partner for the realism of racism isn't something you can do overnight, nor will you be able to make your partner fully understand what it's like to be black in America, but you do owe it to your mate to at least help him or her begin to know the kinds of situations that the two of you may face.

Your partner won't be the only one dealing with new experiences in racism, however. There's a good chance you'll face a new discrimination, and it may come from your own people as well as those outside of your race. Interracial relationships enjoy the distinction of being able to anger whites and blacks equally. Bringing the races together might be a good thing—if only the discontent isn't aimed at you. Consider how you'll handle the possibility of defending yourself and your relationship against brothers and sisters who'll call you a wannabe or a race hater. Then decide if it's something you're willing to accept and deal with in the long run.

FACING YOUR OWN DEMONS

Much as we'd like to believe we're completely open-minded and free of preconceptions and stereotypical thinking, we are not blank slates. In fact, though you may be consciously unbiased in your treatment and expectations of people, you may still harbor an unconscious bias for or against people based on things like—go figure—race. Scientists at Yale University and the University of Washington have found, through a collection of tests known as Implicit Association Tests[1], that most people hold onto unconscious prejudices without ever knowing it. These tests uncover hidden biases that test-takers may have toward other races— or even their own—by measuring their responses to pairings of photos of black people and white people with positive and negative adjectives such as *wonderful*, *agony*, *friend*, *nasty*, *joy*, and *war*. How these biases can affect your life and the lives of those around you may be of little or no consequence in your day-to-day life. But hidden biases can grow and perpetuate, resulting in discrimination.

We've all heard this argument: "I'm not a racist. Some of my best friends are black." While it sounds right in theory, in practice having black friends doesn't necessarily preclude a nonblack person from taking part in racist or discriminatory behavior. It is possible to see past color when you're dealing with individuals one on one and yet see nothing but color when confronted with stereotypes. The same holds true for people of any race, including those in interracial relationships. Personal interactions with people of other races go a long way in healing the rifts that divide us, but in order to truly heal a racist attitude, you must take the lessons you learn from your personal relationships and apply them in a broader way. If you don't, you might be fostering racism despite the fact that your best friend and partner is of another race.

You may be thinking, "What's all this got to do with me?" Now is the time to examine your personal beliefs about interracial relationships as well as any deeply rooted ideologies you may have about white people in general. Once you take the first steps into an interracial relationship, it's easy to forget any negative attitudes you may have held about a particular race. It's also easier to overlook any hate you may be harboring, perhaps as a result of a racist encounter or because of anti-white resentment that your family or friends may have passed along. The same goes for your partner. If she grew up in a household where racist language or actions were the norm, she may be hosting some residual effects from that environment. While these effects may not be obvious in her actions and treatment of others, her subconscious may be quietly acting on their behalf.

According to Tolerance.org (www.tolerance.org), the Southern Poverty Law Center site that hosts the Implicit Association Tests, "Discrimination is based on stereotypes and prejudice that social psychologists believe linger in most of us. Even though we believe we see and treat people as equals, hidden biases may still influence our perceptions and actions."[2]

Racism can affect interracial couples in the most intimate of ways. Imagine being in a relationship with someone for several months or even several years only to find that your views on something are completely divergent. If that something is your favorite color for a sofa or your preferred dessert for Thanksgiving dinner, you probably won't have too much trouble coming to a compromise on the issue, and it probably won't have a negative effect on your relationship. But if the issue is whether or not white privilege exists or whether or not blacks get a fair shake in our criminal justice system, it will probably be much more difficult to move beyond.

Race is a push-button topic that has a tendency to make temperatures rise and tempers flare. Closely examining your own feelings, whether conscious or implicit, can help you prevent ugly surprises at a later stage in your relationship when turning back could be extremely painful. Approaching racial issues doesn't have to be uncomfortable and it doesn't have to be systematic, but being aware of where the two of you stand on certain hot-button issues, especially those surrounding race, will help you identify whether further conversations on the topic are warranted. Relationships can indeed survive, or even thrive, when couples have vastly different views on major issues in their lives. The relationship of rabid Republican Mary Matalin and her husband, Democrat-to-the-end James Carville, comes to mind as one that works despite diametrically opposed political views. In fact, a famous interracial couple, former Secretary of Defense William Cohen and his wife, Janet Langhart Cohen, are in the same situation, as he's a lifelong Republican and she's a lifelong Democrat. But differing views on issues like race take a front-row seat when your partner's view isn't something you can see yourself living with—or passing along to your children.

If an issue divides you and neither of you is willing to change your opinion, discuss how the issue will affect you if you continue the relationship. In some cases, you can come to a compromise on the issue. For example, unless you're both U.S. senators, your arguments about affirmative action aren't likely to affect the future of the policy. In this case, one option could be to decide, as a couple, to sidestep any conversations on that topic. If the issue is one you can accept mutually agreed silence and/or disagreement on, then agreeing to disagree may be your best bet.

It isn't always possible to agree to disagree on fundamental ideological differences, though. According to an article by Coco Helado for Match.com,[3] differences in fundamental beliefs can cause a relationship to crumble. One politically mismatched woman summed up her experiences like this: "One night, we were at a dinner party and [my boyfriend] was arguing against abortion rights. He said it should be illegal. As someone who had had two abortions as a young woman, I found his blanket judgments offensive. All of a sudden I thought, 'This man can never really understand me or my life decisions.'"

If you find yourself questioning your partner's ability to fully understand you and your racial or other fundamental beliefs, or if you have concerns about how your partner's beliefs might affect you or any children you have, think long and hard before moving forward with the relationship.

In the case of implicit biases, the prejudices we apply unconsciously, all is not lost. "There also is preliminary evidence that unconscious attitudes, contrary to initial expectations, may themselves be malleable or subject to change,"[4] according to the Tolerance.org Web site. So, though you may discover, through the Implicit Association Tests or otherwise, that one or both of you has instinctive biases toward one race or the other, you can do something about it. Imaging and exposure to your negative biases may help re-train your psyche, so to speak.

"For example," according to Tolerance.org, "imagining strong women leaders or seeing positive role models of African Americans has been shown to, at least temporarily, change unconscious biases."

Recognizing your hidden biases brings them to the forefront of your consciousness, thus making you aware of areas of your behavior that may be in need of attention and, hopefully, give you incentive to change.

"We would like to believe that when a person has a conscious commitment to change, the very act of discovering one's hidden biases can propel one to act to correct for it. It may not be possible to avoid the automatic stereotype or prejudice, but it is certainly possible to consciously rectify it."

Be thoughtful before you make any rash judgment about your mate based on any implicit biases you uncover, though, because you're likely to find that you've got some hidden prejudices of your own that could use some work.

"WHAT ABOUT THE KIDS?"

If you're thinking of having children in an interracial relationship, "What about the kids?" is a question you will hear frequently. You must examine your and your partner's willingness to commit to giving the best opportunities possible to any children you welcome into your family. Raising biracial children is just like raising any other children, something akin to joining the Peace Corps: it's the toughest job you'll ever love. However, there are race-specific issues that parents of biracial children will face, like multiracial education at schools, children's questions about self-identity, and teaching children to be comfortable with their unique heritage. If you're imagining bassinets and braces in your future, discuss these issues (covered in greater detail in chapter 13) with your mate to ensure you're in agreement. You may not be able to come up with concrete answers about exactly how you'll raise your kids, but at least you won't be flying blindly into the future.

❖ Tracey and Scott's Story

Tracey used to think of herself as "SOUL SISTER NUMBER 1" (with capital letters). Not only would she never have considered dating interracially, she was "completely against interracial dating."

"I exclusively dated within my race. In fact, I was very hostile to and mistrustful of black people who dated outside their race (women and men, but especially men). I had very negative feelings and I was quite vocal about it," she said.

An early childhood experience helped shape Tracey's views on race relations and white people in particular. As an eight-year-old girl in a small racially segregated east Texas town, Tracey was an outsider at her school, with few friends. When she befriended a white girl in her class, she was just glad to have a friend. But that friendship ended the day Tracey overheard her friend's mother telling her daughter that a friendship with a black person was unacceptable.

"At eight years old, I promised myself I would never care about another white person," Tracey admits.

Tracey's reasons for disapproving of interracial relationships changed as she grew older, but her disapproval didn't.

"Most of my concerns had to do with people who dated outside their race as an act of rejecting those individuals within their race. I still have problems with this. I have some concerns about how this may affect biracial children, the children of people who have never dated someone of their same race; for example, a black man who says, 'I hate black women' and only dates white women. To me, there are some deeply ingrained issues of self-hatred that seem to come into play in these kinds of situations."

Tracey's notions about interracial dating began to change after she met Scott, though it did take a lot of convincing. Tracey and Scott met in college. If you ask her, it took three whole meetings before he even remembered her name. He claims it was only two. Either way, it didn't take long before the two of them became buddies. They quickly realized that despite differing skin colors, they had a great deal in common.

"I was very interested in social politics and Scott and I had a mutual love for debate. Our friendship began with simply sharing our views and opinions about the world and life."

That friendship grew, over months and eventually a year, to a point where Tracey stopped seeing Scott as a white man and started focusing on him as just a man.

"Over time, we found ourselves agreeing on issues, and not only on the issues of race. When affirmative action policies were challenged at my university, he understood both the opposing and supporting views. I found myself trying to stump him when it came to race issues. "What do you know about W. E. B. DuBois? What could you know about Marcus Garvey?" Months passed, then almost a year went by.

We started sharing our poetry and other essays. Suddenly I wasn't just dealing with a white man, I was dealing with a man. How could this be, from the girl who practically caused a riot in a mall because a brother walked into a store with a white girl? My friends and family were shocked, and so was I. What was happening to me?"

What was happening was that Tracey was falling in love, though she was reluctant to admit it. And even as she and Scott made the decision to turn their friendship into something more, Tracey still found herself facing those demons from her past.

"I truly had to confront some of my personal prejudices about race when I started dating Scott. I also realized some issues that I had about how I defined beauty. I considered myself to be attractive, but I never thought someone outside my race (other than black men) would also find me as attractive. It took a while for me to become romantically close to Scott because I had all these screwy ideas about interracial dating before I met him."

Yet, according to Tracey, the more she got to know Scott, the less bearing race had on her perceptions of him.

"Each time race could potentially become an issue, it was not an issue, and then it became a non-issue."

Because they had been friends for more than a year when they began dating, making the move into a relationship wasn't fraught with the usual awkwardness that can so often plague the early stages of a relationship. But that didn't preclude the couple from asking all the questions that face interracial couples. Tracey found herself questioning Scott about how their families and friends would handle their relationship and how they as a couple would deal with the reactions of friends as well as the reactions of strangers.

Scott didn't have all the answers, but he was able to reassure Tracey that whatever was to come, they'd face it together.

"From the very beginning of our relationship, Scott told me that if his family refused to respect me as his fiancée, he would never put me in the position to experience mistreatment. In other words, if they couldn't accept me, they couldn't accept him—if they rejected me, they were by default rejecting him. He had resigned himself to the idea that he would sever his relationship with them if it came down to making a decision between his family and me."

Luckily, it didn't come to that. Though there was some initial questioning from both families, the couple now enjoys close relationships with them. And while Tracey and Scott have had a few bumps in the road in their interracial relationship, Tracey finds that they're more like any other couple than they are different.

"We still live one day at a time, handling the prejudice we face as it comes, but honestly, Scott taking out the trash and me balancing the checkbook are usually greater issues."

She still recommends that couples enter into a relationship with their eyes open. "I think for interracial couples, there has to be a conscious decision to count up the costs—so to speak—to evaluate the real challenges that face interracial couples (and you as an individual couple) to determine truthfully and honestly if both people are willing to confront the inevitable/potential struggles together for the sake of the relationship."

3

FACTS AND FALLACIES

WHILE INTERRACIAL RELATIONSHIPS face pitfalls and problems, they are not only about drama and discrimination. Indeed, interracial relationships are more like any same-race relationship than they are different. But because the good stuff—the ordinary stuff—can be, well, ordinary, we often focus on the things that can (and do) go wrong. That's not necessarily all bad, because it's good to anticipate what may lie ahead. The problem is that too much focus on the negative often leaves people believing that the negative is all there is. A case in point: television talk shows.

The thing about talk shows is that the bad ones have a knack for focusing only on what is wrong with our society: "Racist Skinheads and the Women Who Love Them," "I'm Sleeping with My Husband's Brother . . . and I'm Expecting His Child," "I Need a Paternity Test to Find Out Who's My Baby's Daddy." If all you watched was these talk shows, you might believe that all black people dress like Eminem and do jail time, that everyone from West Virginia wears plaid flannel shirts and has bad teeth, that all teenage mothers are bad parents with kids from more than one father, or that all interracial couples have troubled home lives and are always on the verge of splitting up. And while your head knows these things aren't true, when you're caught up in the moment, it's easy to forget.

Beyond the talk show scene, interracial couples are often portrayed in a negative light in the media. On mainstream television and in the movies, interracial relationships are usually riddled with struggle and tension. The critically panned *Save the Last Dance* (2001) saw the lead black character in a fistfight over his white girlfriend. And don't even get started with Spike's *Jungle Fever* (1991); marital infidelity, racism, family drama, lost friends and jobs, and throw in a crack-head brother (played by Samuel L. Jackson), and you know Spike's brewing a recipe for disaster. In the rare instance that an interracial relationship makes the news, it is often unfortunately related to acts of racism or discrimination. An interracial relationship is rarely portrayed as normal and healthy, though that is beginning to change. NBC's *ER* and Fox's *Ally McBeal*, among other television shows, have portrayed interracial relationships without using them as a platform to discuss racial tensions. These shows create a big stir in the interracial community, producing so much excitement that folks like us can be seen as just like everyone else.

A big media setback for interracial couples was the televised O. J. Simpson trial. The media circus surrounding the death of O.J.'s wife, Nicole Brown Simpson, and her friend Ronald Goldman, not only stirred racial tensions around the country, it also created a stereotype that black men abuse their white wives.

Gladys Smith recounted some of the comments she received about her interracial relationship with her husband, Leonard, because of the O.J. trial in an *Africa News Online* article[1]: "It was always: 'Remember O.J. If O.J. beat and killed his wife, Leonard could do the same.' I guess it was the fear that a black man in the company of a white woman was asking for trouble," said Mrs. Smith.

In her book, *Don't Believe the Hype: Fighting Cultural Misinformation About African-Americans*, Farai Chideya systematically debunks the stereotypes about blacks that are perpetuated by media outlets and offers explanations about how and why these stereotypes exist. Chideya tackles such common misconceptions as: "There are more young African American men in prison than in college" and "Drug use is far more widespread among African Americans than white Americans."

"Nearly sixty percent of network news about blacks was negative," Farai reports. In a world where "the vast majority of Americans still live and socialize, if not work, predominantly among people of their own race,"[2] misperceptions of blacks seen on the news can dramatically shape the view of nonblacks who have little or no contact with any African American people.

The same can be said about interracial couples. If the majority of the images of interracial couples we see are the TV talk-show variety, perceptions of mixed-race couples are likely be skewed. It's something of a double-edged sword though, because while it is necessary to bring attention to the issues, too much focus on the problems can backfire and end up perpetuating the stereotypes of interracial couples.

Attention to interracial couples as average or normal relationships is even lacking in the case of scientific research into interracial relationships. As Drs. Leigh Leslie and Bethany Letiecq explain, "Research [on interracial marriages] that does exist typically focuses on problems encountered by interracial couples."

Leslie and Letiecq hope to help remedy the situation with their study on the marital quality of interracial couples. The study "works from an assumption that interracial couples choose their partners for the same range of reasons all other couples select marital partners." And as other research has proven, in most cases, they do.

In this chapter we'll look at several of the facts about and figures on interracial relationships, to debunk some of the hype and also to provide you with a bright side to the problems and pitfalls that will be addressed in future chapters.

Though interracial relationships still make up only a relatively small portion of the population, the numbers are growing and so too should a truer understanding. A good knowledge of the facts and successes of interracial relationships will also provide you with valuable ammunition for shooting down the naysayers.

NUMBERS OF INTERRACIAL COUPLES

The 2000 United States Census found that there are 1.5 million married interracial couples. That's enough people to equal the population of the city of Chicago. Talk about a serious support group!

GROWTH RATE OF INTERRACIAL MARRIAGES

Saying "I do" is becoming increasingly common among interracial couples. In 1960, there were fewer than 150,000 interracial marriages in the United States. The numbers have dramatically increased since then.

A University of Michigan study[3] found that nearly 8 percent of all black men between the ages of twenty-five and thirty-four who were married in 1990 were married to nonblacks. That's roughly 1 out of every 12¼ and a half brothers. White men of the same age are only about half as likely to marry a woman of another race, which puts men like David Bowie in a serious minority. Those same numbers apply to white and black women, who choose to marry interracially at rates of about 3 and 4 percent, respectively. If it looks like black men are setting the trend, don't think that sisters are going to give up that easily: an analysis of government data on mixed-race relationships by Douglas Besharov and Timothy Sullivan for the *New Democrat*[4] found that the interracial marriage rate among black women is climbing faster than the rate for black men.

The rates of interracial intermingling are even greater when you include couples who shack up instead of exchanging vows. The same study found that white women are three and a half times more likely to live with black men than they are to marry them. Fear of commitment, fellas? Maybe you better reread chapter 2.

Of course, with all these figures, there's a catch. Census data tallies the spectrum of interracial relationships, which means that not all of the couples being counted are black/white relationships. Only about 300,000 of the interracial marriages in 1994 involved black/white couples; and a majority of those marriages (around two-thirds) consisted of a black man and white woman.

INCREASING ACCEPTANCE OF INTERRACIAL RELATIONSHIPS

In 1958, the first Gallup Poll conducted on the subject of interracial marriage revealed that 94 percent of whites opposed them. (Surprise, surprise!) Today, acceptance of interracial relationships is growing along with the numbers of relationships themselves.

A 2000 Zogby poll conducted for Reuters found that 67.1 percent of the 1,225 adults polled nationwide said they would approve of their son or daughter marrying someone of another race. Of the approvers, 86.8 percent of black respondents and 62.6 percent of white respondents indicated they wouldn't have a problem with a son or daughter-in-law of another race. (So where are *they* when you're meeting your prospective in-laws for the first time?)

In addition to rising poll numbers indicating a nationwide increase in nods to mixed marriages, other sectors of the population are reporting an increase in acceptance of racially mixed marriages.

According to the *Baptist Standard*, a weekly newspaper of the Baptist General Convention of Texas, Baptist ministers in multicultural communities are seeing the growing trend of interracial marriage reflected in their congregations.[5] With technology making the world a smaller place and folks getting more used to interacting with people of other races on a regular basis, ministers in Baptist churches across the nation are reporting that they see more interracial couples walk down their aisles. Many ministers attribute this trend largely to an increasing acceptance of those marriages. Can I get an "Amen"?

INTERRACIAL COUPLES: RICHER AND SMARTER?

When a reporter asked the folks at Stats.org to assist in finding and analyzing statistics on blacks and interracial marriages, they were initially surprised at the results. "Data appear to indicate that the more educated you are (or the more economically successful you are), the more likely you are to be in an interracial marriage."

Now I'm not so sure what's so wrong with a discovery like that, but apparently the number crunchers figured out that the data they were looking at failed to include age as a variable. I'd be content to forget about age altogether, but in this case, leaving it out makes it look like interracial couples were a lot more successful and smarter than their same-race counterparts. The statisticians concluded that our country's history has as much to do with these findings as anything else, determining that as blacks gained more access to educational and income opportunities, they also gained more access to whites, thus causing an increase in the numbers of interracial love affairs. The numbers were skewed because while older generations were generally less educated and more likely to marry within their race because of racism and segregation, the younger generations were busy breaking glass ceilings and molds alike.

However, it's not enough to dismiss the interracial relationship-success correlation as a historical effect, because more than one study has suggested that age and history alone are not enough to explain the relative successes of interracial couples.

In an analysis of U.S. Census Bureau data, William Frey, a senior fellow of demographic studies at the Milken Institute in Santa Monica and a professor at the State University of New York–Albany, found that "mixed marriages are occurring most among young, higher-income and well-educated individuals."

Further studies suggest that because blacks in higher education have fewer black mates to choose from, they are more likely to choose a mate of another color. With nearly 80 percent of black college students studying in predominantly white institutions, it makes sense that blacks in higher education are more likely to meet, get to know, and date students of other races.

There is also a documented correlation between the level of higher education and the likelihood of marrying outside one's race. In fact, blacks attending graduate school are significantly more likely to marry outside their race than those with only a bachelor's degree.

GROWTH RATE OF MULTIRACIAL BIRTHS

Another good indicator of the rates of interracial unions is the growing number of multiracial people now populating the melting pot. Multiracial births have increased so much in the United States in recent years that the government has had to reexamine its handling of multiracial identification. In 1990, there were about two million children living in mixed-race homes; four times as many as in 1970.[6] Yet, until the year 2000, "check one" was the only option people of mixed-race descent had for identifying their race on a census form. In an effort to adapt to a changing society, the Census Bureau gave 2000 census respondents "the option of selecting one or more race categories to indicate their racial identities."[7] The new "multiracial census" saw 6.8 million people reporting two or more races. Of those, 1.8 million reported being black mixed with at least one other race. The most common racial combination? Black and white.

INTERRACIAL COUPLES AS A MARKER FOR RACIAL HARMONY

Finally, if you're ever in doubt about the bright side of interracial unions, bear this in mind: In addition to the general belief that interracial relationships are one of the best ways to perpetuate the knowledge that the races can coexist without tension, according to *American Demographics* magazine, the increasing number of interracial marriages is challenging the convention of using race and ethnicity to divide our population and serves as an illustration of the "slow, underlying changes in American culture and society" when it comes to race relations.[8]

How's that for changing the world?

4

EXTRA EXTRAORDINARY
COUPLES

INTERRACIAL COUPLES ARE considered outside the mold by much of our society and are still viewed as something of a novelty. This may not seem entirely fair, but even though the numbers of interracial couples in the United States are rising quickly, interracial couples still only account for about 1 percent of the fifty-seven million marriages in the United States.

With numbers like that, it's pretty unlikely to find geographic clusters of interracial couples across this great land, but I'm never surprised when I find interracial couples seeking each other out for socializing and sharing. There's comfort in knowing that others have had similar experiences.

In the beginning of my own relationship, I remember being excited every time I spied another interracial couple at the mall or in a restaurant. It was like validation that we were all right because we weren't the only ones. Back then the Internet was a baby and the only access I had to other interracial couples was via relationships I developed through the now defunct *Interrace Magazine*. Today the world is a much smaller place, thanks to electronic technology, and connecting with couples in similar situations is a great deal easier. For example, I am a member of groups with interests as specific as: black women married to white men, military interracial families, mothers of all boys, work-at-home mothers who write, and subscribers to *Cooking Light* magazine.

Finding people with similar experiences in the age of the Internet can be as simple as the click of a mouse. But what about when a couple has circumstances that make them unique beyond the differences in their races? Minorities within a minority as small as interracial couples will have even greater difficulty connecting with others. And without that connection—which can be so important when you're unlike those around you—couples can end up feeling even more segregated than they are.

Gay and lesbian interracial couples, military interracial couples, and couples who face a sizable age gap in addition to their racial differences all face different sets of challenges when they enter the interracial relationship, as do couples in which one or both partners have children from previous relationships. Complete works can and have been written on each of these topics as they exist independent of an interracial relationship, so I don't intend to give you a comprehensive look at these special circumstances. However, this brief overview will help you discover what it is you need to know about your unique situation.

GAY/LESBIAN COUPLES

In many ways, gay and lesbian interracial couples face a lot of the challenges that heterosexual interracial couples faced decades ago. While the civil rights movement has made things easier on interracial couples, gay and lesbian couples are still largely discriminated against in this country, though things are beginning to change. In addition to the pressures they face as gays and lesbians, gay/lesbian interracial couples will have the added challenge of reconciling the racial issues facing them.

Generally speaking, gay and lesbian interracial couples are more likely to experience approval from within their affinity groups than straight interracial couples. Just as blacks are more likely to approve of interracial relationships because of the discrimination they have over-come, gays and lesbians are more likely to be tolerant of differences. But, even among a generally tolerant community, there can be attitudes of disapproval.

"Interracial relationships? I don't understand them. Or, to be more specific, I don't understand why any Black person would want to become involved in one,"[1] says Talfourd J. Pierce, Jr. in an article for *Blacklight*[2], a webzine for black gays.

"I'm a part of the Black experience and it's a part of me—a part of me I can never share with a White man," he goes on to say.

Pierce's sentiments are no different from those you might expect to hear from any black man who opposes interracial relationships, except that the relationships he speaks of involve black men who love white men.

Colevia Carter, a black lesbian in a relationship with a white woman, was interviewed by *Blacklight* on her experiences in a lesbian interracial relationship. She knows firsthand about attitudes like Pierce's.

"With most of the Black women that I've encountered, it's like I'm all right until they meet my lover. Then they have a visible change in their expression. I think, in interracial relationships, people just don't know what to do with it—particularly in the Black community. It's all nonverbal. They will acknowledge me but they won't acknowledge her. Or they will stare her down and still talk to me."[3]

Outside of the gay/lesbian community, interracial gay and lesbian couples can face the challenge of discrimination on more than one front. Anti-gay sentiments coupled with disapproval of race mixing can greatly increase the intolerance facing these couples. As with all relationships facing adversity, support can be a key factor in ensuring success. Turn to supportive family members or build a family of your own by finding allies among your community. Gay and lesbian support groups, social events, and organizations are more common than similar interracial organizations, so there's a good chance gay/lesbian interracial couples will find support more easily than straight couples.

MILITARY COUPLES

Regular household moves, frequent separation, and the stress of defending one's country can add significantly to the pressures facing a relationship. But despite the increased stresses on military relationships, interracial couples have found something of a haven in the U. S. military services.

A University of Michigan study[4] found that white men who served in the military were three times more likely to marry black women than white men who never served. White women who served in the military were a whopping seven times more likely to be involved in interracial relationships than white women who never served.

The reasons behind the disproportionate numbers of interracial relationships in the military aren't entirely clear, but researchers surmise that the efforts made by the U.S. military to foster healthy race relations within the services following the integration of black forces have had an impact. The U.S. military is probably the most racially integrated large institution in the nation.[5] Indeed, unlike much of the civilian workforce, it's fairly uncommon among military members to have never been in contact with or worked with someone of another race. *The Globalist* reports, "The U.S. military remains one of the few places where blacks routinely supervise and give orders to whites. That makes it a leading-edge institution."[6]

That's not to say that racism in the military doesn't exist, but those with opposing views are probably less likely to voice any discontent.

One nine-year Army veteran, who is interracially married, explained it to me this way: "The military is governed by laws that are strictly enforced. If my white coworker is married to a black woman and I discriminate against him because of it, I'll be punished for that . . . possibly severely. When discriminating against someone because of their skin color means you lose rank or lose your job, you're much less likely to say anything than you might if you were a civilian, even if you do feel that way."

Certainly a number of the interracial marriages in the military are the result of the exposure to different cultures and the availability of partners from different races and countries. The boom in Japanese war brides following World War II is a testimony to that. Since then, it's not uncommon to see interracial military families consisting of one American partner and one from any number of countries around the world that host U.S. military bases. In addition, higher-than-average numbers of minorities in the military, as compared to the population at large, undoubtedly contribute to the increase in race-mixing. For instance, while blacks make up only about 12 percent of the total U.S. population, in the U.S. Army, blacks comprise 36 percent of the highest non-commissioned officers.[7]

Another theory about the numbers of interracial couples in the military is that the freedom from immediate (i.e., geographic) family ties makes entering into an interracial relationship easier for people whose families may not approve of the relationship. In many cases, military service means a steady income, responsibility, and freedom for youngsters who enter the service just out of high school. Without the constant shadow of parental disapproval, and with the increased exposure to the wider world, young people may be more willing or able to date outside of their own race.

Whatever the reason, interracial relationships seem to thrive in the military setting and military interracial couples may deal less with disapproval and discrimination than other interracial couples.

Clayton Majete, a professor at Baruch College, the City University of New York, who has a counseling practice specializing in interracial couples, has summed it up: "For interracial couples, being in the military is better."

MAY–DECEMBER COUPLES

"Age ain't nuthin' but a number . . . " until you bring home someone who is significantly older or younger than you (generally defined as ten or more years) and your family and friends decide that age *does* matter.

So-called May–December romances have long drawn the attention of our society. Older men with younger women get labeled sugar daddies, while older women with younger men are suddenly Mrs. Robinson. It's a critical world for couples with large age gaps, and interracial couples in these situations often face the dilemma of trying to determine the root of any disapproval they're facing.

Some common struggles for intergenerational couples include different social needs, such as ideas how best to spend a Friday night; different maturity levels; and different emotional or professional life positions. When these struggles are added to potential cultural differences, it may be difficult to find a common ground.

Since race issues in our country are viewed differently by each generation, you may find that partners in an interracial relationship who have a great age difference have entirely different views on race—which can create barriers in the relationship. While a child of the mid- to late 1970s might have little to no real life experience with racial discrimination or might only be familiar with the civil rights movement as something from history books, someone just thirteen to fifteen years older may have his or her own memories of Dr. Martin Luther King's assassination and is likely to be much more intimate with racial injustice.

When facing disapproval in this type of relationship, you may question its source. Is it because your mate is a different race or is it because of the gap in your ages? As a relationship ventures further and further away from the norm, the pressure on it has the potential to increase in turn.

Support for age-gap couples is available, from grassroots movements to counselors specializing in these relationships. But you may find that reaching out to both other interracial couples as well as other couples with large age differences will provide you with the information and resources you need to help your relationship flourish.

And remember, relationships where interracial mates have a significant age difference aren't necessarily guaranteed to experience resistance.

Cheryl Gamble-Landrith is a black woman who is married to James Landrith, a white man who is a former U.S. Marine and the editor of *The Multiracial Activist*.[8] Though the couple has many differences between them, none has had a terribly adverse affect on their seven-year marriage, according to Cheryl's comments to PopPolitics.com[9]:

"There are a number of striking differences between my husband and me. Some are obvious. Some are so subtle that the accompanying explanations can take a few minutes. There are differences in politics, religion, tastes, child-rearing philosophies, age, height, weight, hair color, and the one that we barely ever give a thought to—race," Cheryl told the Internet magazine.

Her husband, James, added, "Our differences, however, are not necessarily any greater than those of single-race couples and are not related to race, contrary to what those opposed to interracial marriage would say. Our similarities outweigh any minor differences we may have in our different perspectives on a variety of topics."

INTERRACIAL STEPFAMILIES

Even though the Bradys made it look easy, blending two families into one big happy one can be a task even the ever-resourceful Alice couldn't simplify. And while there are exceptions to every rule, the general consensus among the experts is that bringing two families together takes a lot of love and some hard work.

If the child or children in question are too young to fully comprehend the situation, though you may have to deal with explanations at a later date, you'll probably find that bringing your families together isn't an enormous challenge. Even though both parents might not share a race with the kids, young children of blended families grow up with the benefit of seeing their own family the way we would all like to see society—diverse yet harmonious.

Bringing older children into a new interracial relationship poses the additional challenge of discussing racial issues with them from the get-go. Talking with children about race doesn't have to be complicated, however. When a white or black child is being introduced into an interracial relationship, parents must address questions the child raises about race directly and honestly. Keeping the conversation on the child's level helps you connect with him, and being straightforward helps prevent the child from developing false expectations.

Children generally have less difficulty dealing with racial issues than adults. It's when we burden them with our preconceptions and attitudes that they begin to correlate differences in skin color with differences in how people are viewed and treated by our society.

"Race is an adult notion that means nothing to preschoolers," says Marguerite A. Wright, author of *I'm Chocolate, You're Vanilla: Raising Healthy Black and Biracial Children in a Race-Conscious World.*[10] "Even when they use adult words that refer to skin colors, young children understand these words quite differently. The emotional baggage about race that so many of us carry around does not burden preschoolers."

Share with your child the attitudes about race that are so rampant in our country. Give them the right tools to develop their own views about race. Explain that sometimes people are treated differently because of their skin color and that, indeed, sometimes those people may be their own parents. But let your child know, too, that this kind of treatment is wrong. And don't just tell them it's wrong—tell them why it's wrong. Give them alternatives to discriminatory behavior and give them healthy ways of handling it for themselves. If a child may possibly be teased because his or her stepmother or stepfather is a different race, the child must have a strong sense of him- or herself and a healthy understanding of race.

When it comes to stepparenting in an interracial family, all the standard rules apply. There are a vast number of books and Web sites on the topic of stepparenting, as well as local and national support groups dedicated to assisting blended families. You may find groups aimed at adoptive multicultural families of particular interest. With a recent boom in overseas adoptions, many more families are raising children of a different race or culture than their own. To meet the needs of the growing numbers of these types of families, support groups and clubs are beginning to crop up around the country. Seeking out these groups is a good way to expose yourself to the resources you'll need employ as you journey toward a healthy family that is blended in more ways than one.

And remember, it's love, not biology, that makes a family.

PART II

FAMILY AND FRIENDS

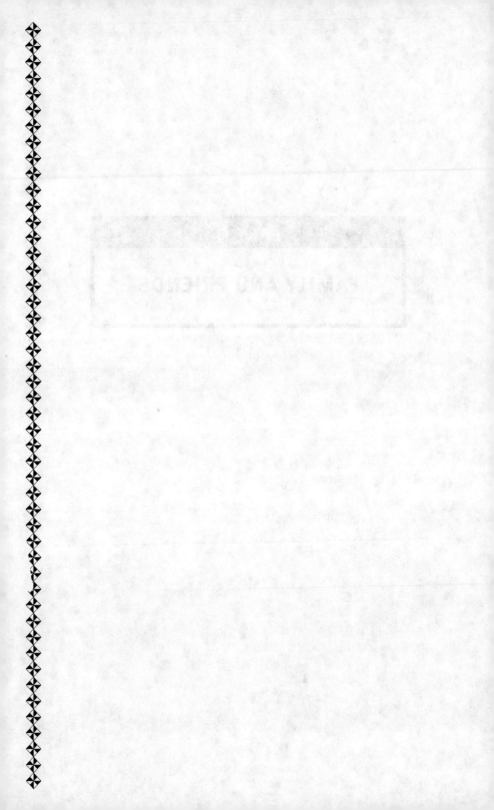

5

YOUR PEOPLE

INTRODUCING YOUR INTENDED TO YOUR FAMILY

When the time comes to introduce your partner to your family, there's bound to be some anxiety all around. Unless you know that your family will welcome your new mate with open arms, you'll have questions and fears about how well they will receive your new relationship. Cultural differences can sometimes lead to uncomfortable situations for you, your partner, and your family. But with a little common sense and some faith—on everyone's part—the meeting might just be the beginning of a beautiful relationship.

Chances are you already have a good feeling about how your family will react to the knowledge that you are in an interracial relationship. Even before the topic is brought to the table, many parents, especially those who oppose interracial relationships, have made their beliefs on the issue known: "No child of mine is going to date a white person." If you know that your parents will disapprove of your relationship, you'll definitely have your work cut out for you in convincing them otherwise, but it's not the end of the world. Overcoming objections isn't always as difficult and dramatic. Many parents are willing to rethink their position on interracial relationships when they're presented with a real-life scenario in their own family.

Psychologist Christine Iijima Hall's fifteen years of experience studying interracial relationships have led her to conclude that black families are historically more accepting of interracial marriages than white families.[1] In fact, a study conducted by Harvard University, the Henry J. Kaiser Family Foundation, and the *Washington Post* found that 86 percent of the African American families polled would welcome a white person into their family with open arms, while only 55 percent of whites would welcome a black person.[2] So the initial meeting with your family will probably be one of the easier introductions you'll make. If you feel sure that your family is among the accepting ones, consider yourself lucky. With at least one set of supportive parents on your side, you and your mate will feel stronger and more capable of facing anyone who disapproves of your relationship.

WHEN PARENTS JUST DON'T UNDERSTAND

Despite the encouraging statistics, some black parents still aren't comfortable with interracial dating. Many black women take serious issue with black men dating and marrying white women, arguing that interracial dating harms black women by reducing the already limited pool of available black men. And, because generational differences can shape racial perspectives, many older black Americans may be less forgiving of interracial relationships. If your parents remember vividly the days of drinking fountains for "coloreds," segregated buses, and civil rights marches, they may be more reluctant to embrace an interracial relationship.

Other arguments against interracial dating are common among blacks who disapprove of these kinds of relationships. Some black people contend that the future of African American culture is at stake. You may hear them say that you have no respect for your race if you choose to date outside of it, or that interracial marriages weaken the black heritage and provide inroads for racism and discrimination. These arguments are largely based on the assumption that black partners in interracial relationships will not pass their own culture to their children or that their children will cease identifying as black, effectively diminishing the numbers of blacks in the country. Diminishment of the numbers, some may argue, will result in less attention being paid to African American and other minority issues that desperately need our society's attention. Contrary to that notion, interracial relationships may actually create allies to the causes affecting blacks and other minorities by introducing more whites to the causes. In fact, a growing number of respected scholars, including Nathan Glazer, Professor of Education and Sociology, Emeritus, at Harvard University and author of the book *We Are All Multiculturalists Now*[3], concede that interracial marriage is one of the most important factors in developing a successful multiracial society in the United States.

Aside from your parents' reactions, you may face opposition from other members of your family. Studies have found that people in interracial relationships tend to rate people of their same race and sex as most supportive of their relationship, and tend to rate people of the opposite sex but same race as most opposed to their relationship. You may find this phenomenon playing out in your own family. While a black man's male relatives may congratulate him on his newfound love, the females in his family might not react so positively to the thought of him dating a white girl. A woman's mother and sisters may be more apt to support her in her interracial relationship while her male kin look disapprovingly on her white mate.

These trends probably don't surprise you. When a sister, even if she's your sister, disapproves of interracial relationships, it's often because she doesn't want to see all the desirable black men being "taken" by nonblack women. Similarly, the brothers, your brothers included, might feel threatened by the loss of a sister to a nonblack man. The threats may seem unfounded considering only about 10 percent of blacks marry outside of their racial group. However, a good portion of those involved in interracial marriages are more educated and successful than those who are not, so the threat of losing the cream of the crop becomes more understandable. Of course, that understanding doesn't justify the opposition you face, but it may make it easier to maintain a level head when defending your relationship. Keeping your cool will go a long way in showing the naysayers that you're mature and serious about your new mate.

If you do find that your parents or other members of your family oppose your new relationship, don't assume this opposition makes them racist. In most cases, any reluctance they express is a manifestation of their love for you and their desire to protect you rather than evidence of racist or discriminatory thinking. Your parents may worry about how society will treat you as a result of your relationship. Or they may be holding onto antiquated stereotypes that prevent them from seeing your potential mate as a person rather than a color. Bear this in mind as you introduce your mate to your folks and try not to be judgmental.

Before the first meeting, consider warming your parents to your cause with some of the evidence in favor of interracial unions discussed in chapter 3. Make sure your parents are aware that interracial couples are much more prevalent in today's society than they were in their generation. The prevalence is not only evidence that interracial relationships are becoming increasingly accepted; it also supports a strength-in-numbers theory.

Vehement opposition and truly racist sentiments from your family are tougher pills to swallow. When parents are so opposed to interracial dating that they'll disown their children who choose an interracial relationship, the stakes climb dramatically. Deciding to pursue the relationship and risk losing your family may be the most heartrending decision of your life, and is obviously one you should consider carefully. Interracial relationships can and do survive without supportive relatives, but be sure that you're ready to give up your family for your relationship before you burn any bridges. (Dealing with the loss of family and friends because of your relationship and seeking out alternate support systems is discussed further in chapter 11.)

Mom, Dad, I'd Like You to Meet . . .

Schedule the first meeting between your parents and your intended after giving your folks fair warning about your relationship. Showing up unannounced with a white lover might result in jaws scraping the linoleum and/or uncomfortable silence. That kind of situation is not fair to your parents or your partner. Share information about your new partner with your family. In addition to telling your parents that, yes, your partner is white, tell them what your mate does for a living, where he or she is from, and how the two of you met, for starters. Also be ready to answer any questions your family might have about the stranger you're about to bring home.

Don't be caught off guard by tough, race-specific inquiries from your family. Whether it's a curious cousin wondering what white guys are really like in bed or a salty sister who wants to know why your girlfriend thinks she's better than the rest of the family, there's a good possibility you'll be asked to reveal information that doesn't fit your definition of need-to-know. Family members may bring up stereotypes about white superiority. In your behind-closed-doors discussions, your responses to these queries can shape your family's view of your mate, so phrase them carefully. Rather than simply dismissing any accusations, give specific examples of how your mate's behavior goes against the stereotypical behavior. Beyond that, trust your instincts—and your partner—and let his or her actions speak for themselves. As for questions about sex, if you wouldn't reveal the intimate details of your bedroom behavior with your family if you were dating a black person, don't feel compelled to share your secrets just because your partner is white. However, if you do decide to kiss and tell, do so with respect to your partner. Giving up the goods isn't fair if it means putting your lover in an uncomfortable situation.

When everyone is on the same page about your budding relationship, it's time to schedule a face-to-face meeting between your parents and your partner. If your family is willing to meet with your intended, chances are they're willing to be won over. Presenting your partner to your family as a person, rather than just a color, is the best way to gain allies.

Consider holding the first meeting on neutral ground, such as a restaurant, where none of you will feel vulnerable or uncomfortable. The first meeting should be brief, but plan a follow-up meeting soon afterward. Since first meetings tend to be somewhat tense, even when there's mutual admiration, a follow-up will help everyone get to know each other without that initial awkwardness.

Prepare your partner for the first meeting by telling him or her a bit about your family. If your family has any unusual quirks (and don't they all?), now is the time to fill your mate in, not after he has embarrassed himself by saying or doing something inappropriate. Remember old Uncle Skeeter from *The Best Man* or John Witherspoon's Mr. Jones character in the *Friday* movies? If there's a similar character in your family, now is the time to come clean. Assure your mate that you'll support him or her throughout the meeting and then follow through, especially if things get uncomfortable. Nothing makes this kind of introduction more difficult for an outsider than feeling as though he or she is standing alone. Above all, be yourself and encourage your partner to do the same. It's an old cliché, but it really is the best way to make a good first impression.

Once you've won your family over, plan on spending time with them on a regular basis. As your relationship evolves, try to include both your parents and your mate's in family activities. Family blending is important in all relationships, but more so in interracial relationships. The more time your families spend together, the better they'll get to know each other and understand the subtle, and not so subtle, differences between your cultures. All of your relationships—and theirs—will strengthen the more they see others as people, rather than as colors.

Beyond the constraints of your immediate families, your relationship has a ripple effect on those around you. According to Phillip Gay, a San Diego State University race-relations expert, "[Interracial couples] commit a whole lot of other people to their marriage and to the whole cause of racial equality and justice. You've got a mother and a father who've got to become more sensitive. Aunts, uncles, and cousins who have to soften. If you multiply those marriages by those who have a stake in it, a lot of people are involved in an interracial marriage." As the people who touch your lives begin to affect the lives of others with tolerant attitudes, society as a whole benefits.

James Allen, a cultural geographer at California State University–Northridge, believes that interracial relationships may actually be a key to a brighter future in race relations.

"I think the ultimate future of America will be very improved by higher rates of racial intermarriage," Allen says. "Racial stereotypes and racism will be much diminished."

Relationships and marriages are not just the joining of two lives, but the blending of two families. By forging strong relationships with your families from the start, you and your mate create a solid foundation for a successful relationship, as well as lead society by example into improved race relations.

❖ Tara and Edward's Story

When Tara and Edward met, it didn't take them long to realize how much they had in common. They both worked as programmers for the same retail company; they shared a love for psychology, art, and music; they were even born in the same month and in the same city! With offices only a few doors away from one another, they quickly became good friends.

But despite all they had in common, there was one difference Tara wasn't immediately able to overlook: their races. When it became clear that Edward wanted the friendship to progress to something more romantic, Tara was wary. She had never dated outside of her race before, so she wasn't entirely comfortable with the idea of a relationship with a white man.

"I actually was hesitant about having a relationship with him because we were of different races. When I could tell he was interested in me, I told him we should just be friends," she admits. Edward, though, wasn't taking "no" for an answer.

"His response was that he would 'convince' me to fall in love with him."

His persistence paid off. The couple eventually began dating, and Tara eventually fell in love with Edward.

As the relationship progressed, the next step seemed inevitable: meeting the parents.

"I wasn't sure how our families would react," says Tara.

Edward's parents are divorced and both have remarried, so the couple planned separate visits to meet his mother and stepfather, and his father and stepmother.

Edward's father's family is no stranger to interracial relationships. His paternal grandfather is white, his paternal grandmother is Hispanic, and his stepmother is black, so telling them ahead of time that Tara was black didn't cause any concern. The couple met with Edward's father and stepmother at Edward's grandparents' house.

For the meeting with Edward's mother and stepfather, the two decided to take a different approach. Since the couple had been taking ballroom dancing lessons, they decided to invite Edward's mother and stepfather to join them at a ballroom dance. The environment allowed the couples to get to know one another while taking the pressure off what could have been an awkward first meeting.

"We went to dinner then dancing and had a nice time. I even danced with his stepfather while he danced with his mother at one point. Conversation was pretty general. We talked about life goals, fears, where we're from, that sort of thing," Tara says.

Tara later learned from a friend of the family that "his grandmother was in tears when she found out Edward was dating an African American." Fortunately, Tara and the family friend had been coworkers, so the friend told Edward's grandmother what a good person Tara is and helped her to look beyond race.

Tara's family supported her from the beginning of the relationship, but they had a few unexpected reactions to Edward's race.

"I told everyone ahead of time that Edward was white. Most gave the same response: 'whatever makes you happy.' My mom did tell me later that my dad said he always knew I was a 'white girl.'"

Tara's sister also voiced some opposition to interracial dating, but in true sisterly form told Tara that it was her decision to make. When Tara took Edward to meet her parents, she chose to invite the rest of the family as well.

"We met at a restaurant along with my sister, brother, and nieces. Edward is pretty good with kids so he spent most of the time talking with them. I don't think he and my dad really know what to say to each other, other than talking about the weather and other small talk like that."

Meetings with extended family members, some of whom didn't know that the couple was interracial, were unremarkable with one exception: Uncle Joe.

"Uncle Joe is a bit of a drunk. Every time we'd see him while we were dating he called Edward 'White Boy.' I would correct him, saying, 'His name is Edward,' but Edward would always say, 'That's alright, he can call me that.' He was a real good sport about it.

"Uncle Joe always jokes a lot with everybody. I wouldn't have accepted anyone in his family doing the same to me. He and Edward did connect because Edward is a good listener. Uncle Joe has his philosophies about life and Edward would always listen and share his thoughts."

Since then, the couple makes it a point to spend time with both of their families. It's easier now, since the couple recently married. The wedding was truly a family affair.

"It was a beautiful wedding. We had help from both sides of the family as far as planning. Edward's mom and stepdad took care of the rehearsal dinner and the cake. His stepmom sang in the wedding and his biracial sister, who is sixteen, was a bridesmaid. His older sister (who is white) was a hostess. My sister was my maid of honor and my dad gave me away. I had three other friends (African American) as brides-maids. Edward had his best friend (white) as his best man, two broth-ers (white), and one friend (African American) in his groom party. We married at the church he and I both [previously] attended. The church is a black Baptist church. We had a traditional wedding with traditional vows and a reception following. The music at the reception was mostly black gospel music. But members of both races danced. A good num-ber from both sides of the family attended the wedding, including fam-ily friends such as his grandmother's childhood friends, which was cool—to have members from the older generation supporting us."

The couple now alternates holidays with each family and spends as much time as possible with both of them. Last Thanksgiving was spent with Edward's family and Christmas was at Tara's family's house. This year they'll flip the script. It helps that their families live in the same areas because Edward is "really into family togetherness," accord-ing to Tara.

"My husband seems to be pretty comfortable when we spend time with my family (or he may not be saying anything about it if he's not). I thought he might have been a little uncomfortable in that first meet-ing. But since then he talks to them more when we're with them. We play a lot of card games in my family so that usually helps to loosen things up. But I find that I am not quite comfortable yet spending time with his family. It may go back to my being uncomfortable being around all white people and I'm the only black in the crowd. It's taking me longer to really connect, I guess," Tara admits.

Plenty of family interaction will give Tara more opportunity to connect. The families now get together in a larger group, rather than the couple visiting each family separately.

When asked to offer some advice to other interracial couples who are feeling out family situations, Tara offers:

"Tell family ahead of time that your partner is of another race! Do not assume they will be pleasantly surprised. Depending on how sensitive your partner is, the first meeting may already be awkward, without the element of surprise and the initial reactions that come with it."

Tara is hopeful that things will get easier for interracial couples in our society.

"I think the times are changing. More people have had at least some association with people of other races and it's becoming less of an issue, or at least people are more tolerant or not so outwardly opposed to it."

6

THEIR PEOPLE

MEETING YOUR INTENDED'S FAMILY

If you thought tackling the introductions of your partner to your family was stressful, now it's your turn to meet your intended's family—and they don't know and love you like your own family.

You have good odds of being accepted by your mate's family. According to polls, about three out of five white families would approve of their child dating interracially. However, pollsters admit that there's no way of knowing how many of those agreeable whites are just saying they'd approve of a nonwhite son- or daughter-in-law in an effort to seem liberal. Finding out whether your potential in-laws are truly accepting or just trying to be politically correct can be tricky.

The reasons that whites disapprove of seeing their children in interracial relationships usually fall along all the same lines as any kind of racial discrimination. Two common reasons are:

1. An inherent belief that their race is superior to other races,

   and

2. The fear that their child will face discrimination because of the relationship.

It's no surprise minority-hating, racist white parents hit the roof when their baby brings home a black girlfriend or boyfriend. The surprise comes when family members appear to be tolerant of differences and then suddenly change their tune when their child brings home a nonwhite date. You know the situation; they're the family whose daughter's black best friend has been around for years, coming over for dinner and sleepovers without so much as a mention of her race. But they quickly start singing a different tune when the same daughter wants to take a black guy to the prom. Such families feel completely justified in their feelings because, after all, they're not racist; they're just trying to protect their child from a racist society.

Arguments like these are painfully common among parents who disapprove of interracial relationships. And though such arguments are wrong on every level, you must try to step back from the injustice of it all and consider the reasons a white parent may resist the thought of their child being in an interracial relationship. Doing this will help you understand their opposition and help you and your partner make a more convincing argument for your relationship.

You know that blacks have been and continue to be misrepresented in the media as drug-dealing, welfare-receiving, thug criminals. While the media is making efforts to change their portrayal of blacks, the damage has already been done. Some whites who have had no other contact with black people or exposure to black culture other than the media might start believing such propaganda. Put yourself in the same shoes: if you never had the opportunity to visit the state of Utah, for example, based on media representations of people who live there, you might assume that they are all hyper-religious, conservative, white Mormons who believe in polygamy and home-schooling their children. Media representations of unknown cultures and people are so powerful that it's easy to buy into them when you don't have any firsthand experience from which to draw your own conclusions. Now, should you be lucky enough to meet a hip and trendy Utah native and get to know her, you'd be far less likely to lump her into your preconceived notion of what people from Utah are all about.

Use this information to your advantage as you and your mate decide how and when to approach his or her parents with your budding relationship.

The first step, informing the family about your interracial relationship, is one your mate should take alone. Since sparks may fly as a result of the announcement, it's best to keep it strictly a family affair. This way you're much less likely to immediately be perceived as the enemy, and because your partner knows his parents better than you do, he's better equipped to handle any drama that may follow. For the initial proclamation, be sure your partner is well prepared to counter any attack his or her parents may launch. Your partner should relay all the positive things you've each gained from the relationship as well as the encouraging statistics about interracial relationships (see chapter 3). Having a game plan before you drop "the bomb" is important. Your mate must let the family know he or she has thought the relationship through and isn't entering into a potentially sticky situation with eyes closed. He or she should explain that you're both aware of the obstacles that will face you in the future and that you're willing to face those obstacles together. Incidentally, approaching your partner's parents with this kind of preparation will serve you both well whether you're expecting the family to disapprove or not.

Beyond the fear of how their child will be treated because of the relationship, parents may also be concerned about any backlash they may face. Parents may worry that other family members will chastise them for *allowing* their child to pursue a relationship with a black person. Or they may fear being ostracized by friends or colleagues who disapprove of race-mixing. Parents who feel this way may not vocalize this apprehension to their children, but knowing that it might exist may help you to understand and possibly alleviate some of their apprehension.

If the family is completely resistant to the relationship and is prepared to disown their child or forbid him or her from seeing you, you and your partner have to make some tough choices. One option is choosing to end the relationship rather than face ongoing struggles. But if you and your mate aren't willing to end the relationship, you face two

alternatives: living with the family's rejection or keeping the relationship secret. Neither is perfect, but desperate times sometimes call for
imperfect solutions. While I don't normally advocate secrecy, it may be
the only solution when your partner's family will not accept the relationship, and your partner is committed to maintaining a relationship
with his or her family despite their bigotry. Keep in mind that a secret
of this magnitude can cause major stress on your relationship, com-
pounding the other stresses you'll face as an interracial couple.

If you choose to learn to live with intolerant in-laws, you'll face
many challenges. Ways of dealing with ongoing opposition and disapproval from friends or family members are discussed at length in chapter 11. While exceptionally bigoted in-laws will simply opt to have
nothing to do with you, some disapproving families eventually change
their tune about a child's interracial relationship. Many parents decide
that seeing their son or daughter is far more important to them than
opposing the interracial relationship, and they will make an effort to get
to know their child's partner. In other instances, the birth of grandchildren will cause a stubborn grandparent to rethink his or her opposition to the relationship. Though you shouldn't base a decision to
proceed with a relationship on the hope that opposing family members
will eventually come around, stranger things have happened.

The next step is meeting your intended's family and getting to
know them. Meeting the parents is one of the most nerve-racking
moments of any relationship. How else could entire sitcom episodes be
built around the event? If you've been in other serious relationships,
interracial or otherwise, you already know what to expect as you prepare to meet the parents. The idea of being scrutinized as "good
enough" or "not good enough" for someone's beloved son or daughter
is enough to make even the most self-assured feel overly conscious of
his or her behavior. We all want to do the right things, say the right
things, and make a good impression. There's no room for social gaffes
or blunders, or at least it doesn't seem like there is. When you're in an
interracial relationship, however, the potential for rejection goes beyond

how you behave to the simple color of your skin. Blacks in interracial relationships with whites are often burdened with the unfortunate responsibility of representing their entire race when they face their partner's parents. If your mate's parents have preconceived notions about blacks, they may be looking to you to dispel those myths. All you need to do is put your best foot forward and be yourself. Resist any urge to dress in gang attire, practice your Snoop Dog-isms, or show off your extensive Ebonics vocabulary. If you feel you must go hip-hopping through your future in-law's front door, you deserve whatever is coming to you. I'm not suggesting that you be anything but yourself, but I am recommending that you be the very best self you can be.

Here are some dos and don'ts to bear in mind during the initial meeting.

1. **Do** remember that you're all in the same boat, even though it might feel like you're completely on the spot.

    Everyone will be nervous about this first meeting, including your partner's parents. Try to keep that in mind so that you don't feel like the only remaining contestant on *Survivor* on vote night.

2. **Don't** go overboard trying to break the ice.

    Keep conversation light and avoid any potential hot-button issues such as politics or religion. It's bad enough having the big pink elephant of race sitting on the table; don't add fuel to the fire.

3. **Do** defer to your partner when faced with any pointed questions that you aren't sure how to respond to or if you feel particularly put on the spot.

    Your partner is better equipped to handle his or her own parents if the situation starts to get sticky.

4. **Do** remember that you and your mate are on the same team.

    Presenting a united front will help both of you feel more comfortable and will send the message to the parents that you're in it together.

5. **Don't** go into the situation with resentment or a chip on your shoulder.

   Now is not the time to be boiling about the injustice of racism and discrimination, no matter how appropriate the feelings may be. For the sake of your mate and your relationship, make every effort to put aside your anger at the idea of being judged by your skin color. That's not to say that you should excuse any racism exhibited by your partner's family, but do try to give your mate's parents the benefit of the doubt—at least this time.

6. **Do** ask questions of your future in-laws.

   Focus some of the conversation on the parents rather than you, the couple, to allow for a break in the pressure and to show the family that you're as interested in them as they are in you. Ask your mate's mom about her job or her interests or make an effort to get dad into a conversation about the local sports teams.

7. **Don't** forget to include any siblings who may be present in conversations and activities.

   If younger brothers or sisters are present, relate to them on their level about things they're currently involved in. If the sibs are older, share some personal things about yourself and invite them to do the same. Supportive siblings can be a great ally in your fight to win over the parents, and because they're often of the same generation as you, they're more likely to be tolerant and accepting of interracial relationships.

8. **Do** remember to thank your partner's family if they've hosted you in their home or if they've footed the bill for the day's activities.

9. **Don't** forget to suggest a repeat performance, even if the encounter wasn't all you'd hoped it would be.

Letting the family know that you're committed to spending time with them, with their child, shows that you're willing to reach out to them and that you plan on being around for a while.

Winning over your partner's parents might not be your idea of a fun night out, but developing a good relationship with your mate's kin is important. It alleviates the pressures on your relationship and helps to establish a strong support system in the months and years to come.

✦ Brenée and Bryan's Story

Most parents would be thrilled at the idea of their child meeting and marrying someone from the same church. The notion of your child sharing a life with someone of the same faith should be comforting. But when Bryan's family found out that he and his friend Brenée had intentions that weren't just platonic, they were anything but comforted.

Bryan and Brenée met as teenagers when Bryan and his family moved to town and joined Brenée's church. The two hit it off immediately and quickly became the best of friends. The fact that he is white and she is black seemed of little consequence to anyone, including Bryan's parents.

"When Brenée and I were 'just friends,' I won four free tickets to a concert in town. Being that Brenée was my closest friend, I asked her to join me. The other two tickets I gave to my mother to do with as she wished. We all decided to ride together since we didn't really know the general area of where the concert was being held. My mom and Brenée hit it off really well. My mom even mentioned how pretty she thought Brenée was," Bryan says.

A year into their friendship, Bryan finally mustered up the nerve to ask Brenée out. To his delight, she accepted and the two became inseparable. Even at the young age of eighteen, Bryan had some experience with interracial relationships—and his family's reaction to them.

"Growing up, I never thought much about [interracial relationships] until my parents made a big deal about it when I dated one of the local pastor's daughters, who happened to be a very light-skinned black girl. I was about sixteen or so at the time, and my parents forbade it because they claimed they weren't prejudiced, they just wanted to protect me from those who were."

Despite his parents' previous reactions to interracial relationships, the fact that they rejected Brenée without ever really getting to know her wore heavily on Bryan.

"When we began dating, my parents wouldn't allow me to bring Brenée over to the house. Without knowing much about her, other than the first time my mom met her, they wanted nothing to do with her." Bryan was not even allowed to talk about Brenée at his parents' house.

However, because Bryan was living away from home at college, his relationship with Brenée was able to flourish despite his parent's objections. Over the next couple of years, Bryan and Brenée continued to see one another against his parents' wishes. "Yes, they were aware that we were dating and quite in love," Bryan said. "They just didn't want to hear about it, talk about it, or even see it.

"For two and a half years my parents refused to acknowledge her. I was in college at the time, so their threats didn't go very far."

But while his relationship with Brenée flourished, Bryan's relationship with his parents was crumbling. And suddenly, so was his father's health.

Two and a half years into his relationship with Brenée, Bryan received an urgent call from his mother informing him that his father had pancreatic cancer. The family realized that time was too precious to waste and in the following few months spent their time together "focusing on the things in life that really mattered."

"Toward the end of my father's life, my parents allowed Brenée to come over to the house for a few very formal dinners. It was awkward for both parties, but at least it was a positive step in the right direction.

"I think Brenée was extremely nervous because of what she already knew of my parent's unfair prejudice toward her. I prepared her as much as I knew how to interpret my family's body language, common phrases, etc."

When I asked Bryan if the couple had lost any friends or family as a result of their relationship, the only one he mentioned was his father.

"I can't say that our relationship had a direct impact on his cancer, but from day one, my father used to say when he thought about my future with a black woman, it 'tore at his gut.' He spent so much time worrying about me."

Soon after his father's death, Bryan's mom "did a complete turnaround." Since then she and Brenée have even taken a cruise together to get to know each other better.

As for Brenée's family, they've welcomed Bryan into the fold with open arms from the beginning. Bryan recalled the first time he met Brenée's family. "We had been 'dating' for less than a month, but had become close friends over the past year. We were pretty serious about each other, and Brenée wanted to introduce me to her entire family. She knew that the annual Fourth of July cookout at her uncle's house would provide the greatest opportunity.

"I guess I made a good impression because the next time I saw them all again, it was Christmas time at her aunt's, and they were all asking me how to pronounce my last name. 'Brenée Dihigo has a ring to it!' they said. I guess that was their way of saying, 'Son, you're family now.'"

Brenée did take Bryan's last name, eventually. The couple waited five years before they married. They chose a five-hundred-year-old Spanish fortress in Puerto Rico as the locale for their wedding.

"We opted to do something different because even though we met in church, we felt that after going through hell with my parents, we just wanted to get away—to paradise, in fact."

But an escape to an island paradise wasn't the only benefit to having a destination wedding. When I asked if any friends or family members refused to attend the wedding, Bryan admitted:

"We knew that we would 'weed out' a lot of people by having it so far away, and we did. The only ones who would come would be the ones who really cared and supported us. And they did!"

Since then the couple has been working hard at the business they started together and just enjoying their status as newlyweds.

"We love being married. We felt we did it the right way. College then marriage. We didn't want to rush into things even though we knew from the beginning that we were meant to be."

Even their respective families have formed relationships.

"My mother and Brenée's mother have developed a good friendship."

As for advice the couple would offer to other couples in similar situations, Bryan had this to say: "Don't try to conform to what the parents expect you to be (or even want you to be) because you could possibly spend your entire life trying to 'fit' their ongoing expectation. Just be yourself."

PART III

WHERE IN THE WORLD?

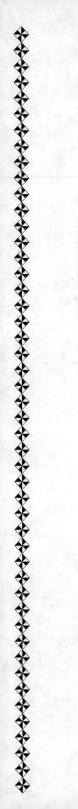

7

LOCAL AND REGIONAL FLAVOR

LOOKING FOR HOME sweet home? Settling on a place to settle down is a big decision for any couple. When you're both from the same hometown, you have common ideas about what you're looking for in a home. But couples from different corners of the United States might find themselves at odds over where to lay down roots. Interracial couples face the added challenge of finding a home that won't leave them worrying about getting lynched while mowing the lawn or with neighbors who may decorate the front yard with a burning lawn ornament in the shape of a cross. OK, so those are overly dramatic examples. In reality, interracial couples can and do make happy homes in all parts of our great country. But it's common to have questions about how well received you and your relationship will be in a new place.

ASK THE JONESES?

When you're checking out a new place to live, though you might love the way a certain house or neighborhood looks, there are no surefire ways to gauge the livability of a place at a glance. Asking current residents how nice a neighborhood is seems like a good place to start, but you may want to think twice before you go knocking on doors to quiz strangers.

Trying to get people to talk frankly about racial issues is tricky. Getting folks to talk about any racial tensions they're living with might be darn near impossible. They know Mr. Jefferson up the street calls Mr. Willis next door "Whitey," but they probably won't tell you that. In fact, even if you can get people to discuss their local race relations, some studies suggest that people may be wearing rose-colored glasses when it comes to their perception of the racial situation on their block.

In conjunction with their six-week series entitled "How Race Is Lived in America,"[1] the *New York Times* asked 2,165 adults questions about their perceptions of race in the United States. Among other things, the surveyors concluded that peoples' perceptions about the state of race relations generally improved as the questions literally hit closer to home.

Susceptible perhaps to the pressures of political correctness, [respondents] seemed to strive to depict themselves and their neighbors as open-minded and accepting while projecting less enlightened views on the rest of the country. And the farther from home, the worse things seemed. For instance, 88 percent of whites and 82 percent of blacks said race relations were generally good in their neighborhoods. Similarly large majorities of whites and blacks said race relations were generally good where they worked and at their children's schools. But the numbers dropped when people were asked to characterize race relations in their communities, and they dropped more precipitously when they were asked about race relations in the country. Fifty-eight percent of whites and 51 percent of blacks said race relations in the country were generally good, while 30 percent of whites and 40 percent of blacks said they were generally bad.[2]

While being politically correct may be the best way to make sure you don't tick your neighbors off, it doesn't always tell the true story about how nice it is to live somewhere. And when you're thinking about moving, that's what you really need to know.

So if asking the neighbors race questions isn't going to get the job done, how about just looking at them? Checking out the racial makeup of a neighborhood might also seem like an elementary place to start your research, but if the respondents to that same poll are accurate, many neighborhoods are more racially homogeneous than you might be seeking.

While racial discrimination—past and present—explains much residential segregation, personal preference also plays a role, too, according to Kelvin M. Pollard and William P. O'Hare of the Population Reference Bureau:

> A study of Los Angeles residents found, for example, that most minorities prefer to live in areas where their ethnic or racial group makes up at least 40 percent of the population. Public policies have sought to end involuntary segregation, reflecting the consensus that discrimination in housing harms society, but there is less agreement about whether voluntary segregation is detrimental.
>
> Racial differences in perceptions of what constitutes an integrated neighborhood may also sustain residential segregation. Demographer William Clark[3] found, for example, that blacks in several large cities preferred neighborhoods that were equally divided among blacks and whites. Most whites preferred an integrated neighborhood as well, but one where 80 percent of the residents were white and just 20 percent black.[4]

The previously mentioned *New York Times* poll also found that though 85 percent of whites said they "did not care" who their neighbors were, some 67 percent said they believed that most white people preferred to live in areas where they were surrounded by other whites. Further, a full 85 percent of the whites polled also said that the neighborhoods they lived in had no or few blacks living there. Startling though those numbers, and the contradictions therein, may be, I'm going to push the envelope a bit and suggest that it's a basic human instinct to desire to be surrounded by a community of people like you.

Now, whether "like you" means of similar income, or interests, or race may depend on the situation you're in, but in a room full of strangers, there's no denying that color tends to be the simplest common denominator when people are seeking to identify with others like themselves. Beyond that, when it comes to race, there is a certain safety in being surrounded by folks who look like you. The feeling is, though you may have nothing else in common, at least if we share the same skin color, you can't dislike me because of that.

We've all experienced it. You walk into a party, a restaurant, or a shopping mall with your mate and are immediately struck by the fact that you're the only black person in the place. Whether or not this discovery unsettles you, you know as well as I do that as soon as you locate someone else who looks like you, you feel less alone and somehow at least a tiny bit more comfortable.

In her book *Why Are All the Black Kids Sitting Together in the Cafeteria?*[5] author Beverly Daniel Tatum discusses exactly this phenomenon. As an authority on race relations, Tatum has examined race, racism, prejudice, and stereotypes on many levels and has shared her understanding of the "cafeteria phenomenon." Tatum explains, "Different groups have different needs, and people of color have a strong need for connection and empowerment."

She calls the grouping of races in these social situations "affinity groups"—safe spaces that allow individuals to positively explore their identities among their peers. She feels that participation in these affinity groups allows individuals to develop the skills necessary for participation in larger, more diverse groups:

> The shared goal in making affinity groups available is to interrupt the cycle of racism. For white people, this might involve processing their reactions to racism: typically, shame and guilt. For people of color, it might be anger. Affinity groups also help individuals participate in larger, blended groups. They are good for overall community-building.[6]

So while it might not seem ideal, the act of "sticking to one's own race" does fulfill certain social development needs.

But what does all this mean for interracial couples? Interracial couples, by definition, are the antithesis of this hypothesis within their relationships: not seeking out their affinity group, but, in fact, going against it. As a couple, however, it isn't uncommon for interracial couples to seek out other interracial couples with whom they can relate, socialize, and share experiences—looking for affinity groups of our own. But when we move beyond the cafeteria to neighborhoods or towns, seeking out concentrations of interracial couples isn't as easy as finding a predominantly white/black/Hispanic neighborhood. Because while an interracial utopia might look to you like streets lined with multiracial children playing hopscotch and moms and dads of different races from each other barbecuing, baking cookies, and driving car pool, the likelihood of finding a community that is predominantly interracial couples is slim. Of course, it isn't necessary to live solely among other interracial couples in order to make a happy, comfortable home.

For starters, predominantly black neighborhoods can be an excellent choice for the interracial couple who is looking for tolerance and acceptance. Statistically speaking, black neighborhoods will be more welcoming of an interracial couple, and the couple may well feel more at home among minorities. You may also find that not only do you feel more comfortable in a black neighborhood than you might in a white one, but your spouse may feel more comfortable there as well. What's more, your children will benefit from greater exposure to black culture, which, face it, is harder to come by day to day than the whiter side of life.

That's not to say that you should rule out whiter neighborhoods, though. Face it, there are more white people in our country, so there are more white neighborhoods to be found. And while there's no doubt that some 90-percent white towns would be the last place on earth you'd want to lay roots, you might find a predominantly white community that is known for its tolerance and diversity that is the perfect place for you.

So how do you go about finding the perfect place for your family?

IMMERSE YOURSELF

Don't spend all of your time in a potential new neighborhood just looking at houses. To find the perfect place for your family, take some time to get a feel for the neighborhood. Eat dinner at the local fast food joint or neighborhood restaurant. Check out the patrons as well as the restaurant staff. Do they represent a racial mix you're comfortable with? Next, hit the shopping malls. Observe the other shoppers and the folks who are ringing up your purchases. Are you getting odd stares? Are there other blended couples? Along the same vein, drop by the local supermarkets and drugstores. There, in addition to observing the people, look at the products. If there are no relaxers or hair grease in sight, let that be a clue to you. At the grocery store look for culture-specific foods. A wide range of ingredients for various ethnic cuisines is indicative of a culturally diverse environment.

While you're driving, turn on the radio. The music and talk radio available may give you an indication of the local demographic.

GET WIRED

Knowledge is power, right? Well, seek ye out your strength. The Internet provides a wealth of resources for couples looking to make a move. Despite the looming digital divide that finds many blacks with less access to computers—and less likely to use the computers they've got—getting on-line may be the best way to find the information you need to choose your next place of residence. Using the Internet to research potential places to live will save time and money by eliminating some long distance phone calls and traveling.

Here are some things to be on the lookout for while you surf the Web.

Population Breakdowns

The U.S. Census Bureau's Web site (http://quickfacts.census.gov/qfd) allows you to search geographically for the racial population makeup of specific regions. While this doesn't help much in terms of getting to know your neighbors, it can give you a clue about which areas of a state house the most minorities and the highest racial diversity. Knowing that there are races other than white in a potential new city gives you at least some information to start with. If a town's population breakdown shows 98 percent white and 2 percent other, you might not feel as comfortable there as in a town with a higher minority to majority ratio. You can also compare these statistics with the statistics of your current city, which may surprise you. Noting how the numbers relate to your city's diversity will give you an idea of how to employ this new information.

Regional Flavor

Many sites bring the flavor of their cities to locals and to those considering a visit or a more permanent move to the city. In addition to a wide network of Web sites run by city governments, sites like DigitalCity.com, CitySearch.com, and Yahoo's Get Local (http://local.yahoo.com) offer a glimpse at local culture by providing articles, reviews, forums, and events calendars on-line. Some sites even include links to local radio stations that stream their broadcasts. Take a peek at what the city you're considering has to offer and see if the local flavor appeals to you. Use this insider's opportunity to take notes on the city's regular happenings and to read some of the locals' reviews of the areas' events. Evidence of, say, an upcoming African arts festival or weekly ethnic food markets can give you an idea about the kind of environment you're considering. Also, take advantage of the message boards and chat rooms at these local sites. Post questions you may have about the city, or even specifically ask if the city is interracial-relationship friendly. You'll have the benefit of a wide variety of responses from many people, which you can use to gauge how comfortable you might feel in the city. Alternatively, you might try to corner a local resident in a chat room to get real-time answers to your questions.

Organizational Presence

There are several organizations aimed at supporting interracial couples and multiracial families across the country. The home bases of these organizations can serve as a tip-off about the supportiveness of the communities. Many of these organizations are happy to answer your questions about the city in which they're located. For example, the Interracial Family Network of Seattle–King County offers to e-mail a list of recommended communities to interracial couples considering a move to the area.

Beyond interracial-specific organizations, you may wish to check out local chapters of organizations aimed at specific minority groups, such as the NAACP. Even if you don't have an interest in joining one of these organizations, the knowledge that they exist in your new city can give you some peace of mind that there are enough like-minded people to support the presence of such organizations.

Job Opportunities

Unless you are moving for a new job, you may need to find a job when you arrive at your new destination. The obvious on-line resources for job searching are essential, but some sites, particularly IMDiversity (www.imdiversity.com), specialize in job resources for various ethnic minorities. At IMDiversity you can post your resume, search available jobs, and learn more about diversity-sensitive employers in your area.

The Ugly Stuff

Much as we loathe admitting it, hateful, ugly people do exist. And let it be known that they are apt to congregate. Luckily, there are a few good resources for seeking out regions that hate groups call home base. Avoid the hate group hot spots by checking out the on-line sites of hate group watchdog organizations like Hatewatch.org, the Southern Poverty Law Center's Intelligence Project (www.splcenter.org/klan-watch.html), and the Anti-Defamation League (www.adl.org). These types of groups, and their accompanying Web sites, can be invaluable tools. For instance, the Southern Poverty Law Center's site allows you to search its database of 676 active hate groups in the United States by type of hate group as well as by state.[7] The state-by-state listings tell you which hate groups are in the state and in which specific cities they are located—a valuable tool for narrowing down the possibilities.

Another extremely useful tool is the National Criminal Justice Reference Service (www.ncjrs.org/hate_crimes/hate_crimes.html). Their section on hate crimes provides not only information regarding hate crime laws and definitions, but also resources and links (www.ncjrs. org/hate_crimes/additional.html) to information about hate crimes by location. One of the resources listed is the FBI's Uniform Crime Reporting Program (http://www.fbi.gov/ucr/ucr.htm), which is the nation's only comprehensive crime data collection program. This site contains the agency's annual published reports on hate crime statistics in the United States, which includes breakdowns of reported hate crimes across the country by city, state, and motivation. While these resources can be a bit startling and intimidating, they are invaluable to a couple in need of the information to help keep them safe.

Another benefit of doing your research on-line is the anonymity of the Internet. Being colorless in cyberspace allows you to communicate candidly with locals in your new city without divulging personal information. People may be more likely to spill the truth about race relations in their city, especially the not-so-nice things, in the nonconfrontational atmosphere of on-line interaction than they would be in a face-to-face discussion.

UNDERSTANDING REAL ESTATE LAWS

When you're moving, the last thing you need is another headache. In an effort to keep the move simple, you may choose to enlist the assistance of a professional. Whether you're planning to buy or rent a home, a reputable real estate agent can save you a lot of time and hassle. Scanning the classified ads is OK if you're moving to an area you're familiar with, but if you're moving to a new city or state, you may find that the classifieds don't provide enough information about potential residences.

Finding a real estate agent is generally the easy part; getting information from that person regarding the livability of a place can be more difficult. Additionally, there are a few things to keep in mind as you proceed with house hunting with the assistance of a real estate agent.

While the first thing on your mind as an interracial couple may be the city's racial makeup and how well you will be received, equal opportunity laws prevent agents from divulging information about the racial makeup of a neighborhood, city, or town—even if you come right out and ask them. These laws, which fall under the Fair Housing Act of 1968, are good because they prevent racial discrimination in the sale of housing. But as a couple with a unique interest in the racial climate of a potential new city, the laws make it a challenge to get the information you need. So, although your intentions may very well be in your own best interest, any discussion about the racial makeup of a neighborhood can land the agent in a heap of trouble.

Real estate agents who are found guilty of any of the following practices can lose their license and more, and therefore will steer clear of anything that could be perceived as an inappropriate discussion about a property they're showing.

- Racial Steering: Includes showing houses in certain locations only to whites while showing other locations only to minorities.
- Blockbusting: Representing a neighborhood as deteriorating (because its racial or ethnic composition is changing) in order to cause panic selling of houses.
- Blatant Refusal to Rent or Sell: The refusal to rent or sell an available apartment or house on the basis of race, such as falsely telling a black person that a house or apartment has been sold and then showing it to a white person.
- Redlining: The refusal of banks and insurance companies to approve mortgages or insurance in predominantly minority areas.
- Price Modification: Quoting one price or rent to whites and another to minorities.[8]

If you believe you've been a victim of such practices, contact a lawyer, who can help you determine if your agent has in fact acted in a discriminatory manner and help you determine the appropriate action to take. Conversely, bear these practices in mind before you put your agent in an uncomfortable position, and possibly embarrass yourself, by pressing him or her with racial questions.

Word to the wise and off the record: A black real estate agent may save you some legwork by being more understanding of your desire to find a racially comfortable community, without your having to voice that desire.

❖ Monique and David's Story

When Monique and David decided they were ready for a change of pace from their Washington, D.C., life, it was a mutual decision.

"We wanted a change. We wanted to live somewhere new. We both have lived most of our lives in the Washington, D.C., area, so we wanted to live somewhere new and try something different," says Monique.

Exactly where was something they weren't as sure of. While the couple knew what qualities they were looking for in a new locale—"diversity, housing [prices], weather, things to do"—they weren't sure what area of the country would best suit them. David is an aspiring screenwriter, so the opportunities available to him in Hollywood made it an obvious option, but the couple was determined to size up as many cities as possible before making a final decision.

After an initial survey of their options and the cities they would consider living in, the couple narrowed their selections down to several choices: Tampa, Florida; Chicago, Illinois; Detroit, Michigan; Boston, Massachusetts; and Los Angeles, California.

When it was feasible, the couple worked trips to potential cities into their plans, to experience firsthand what each of the areas had to offer. One by one, the couple eliminated cities for a variety of reasons: Boston was out because of the cold climate and the high cost of living.

Tampa didn't make the cut due to a combined lack of diversity and things to do. And despite having grown up in Motor City, Monique decided that Detroit was too racially segregated and couldn't offer the diverse neighborhoods the couple was seeking for their future children.

"Diversity has always been on the top of our list for places to move to," according to Monique.

The couple utilized the Internet to research the places they couldn't visit and to get additional information about the places they did see. As Monique tells it, "The Internet played a lot in our research. We tried our best to visit every place we considered moving to but that can financially add up."

After seeing what each of their choices had to offer, the couple finally settled on Los Angeles as their destination. Los Angeles had been a dream city for the two of them since they'd been a couple. After visiting in 1999, the couple came away from the city with a good impression. Though the cost of living was higher than they might have liked, the weather suited them, the people seemed nice, there were a lot of things to do there, and the diversity of the city pleased them. Add that to the abundant opportunities for screenwriters in the area and the decision seemed elementary.

They followed up their visit with more Internet research, including visits to sites like realtors.com and brochures ordered from Los Angeles–based Web sites. They supplemented that with books on the local area and moving guides designed specifically for those interested in moving to Los Angeles.

Unfortunately, despite diligent research, the couple still found the move to be "a huge culture shock!" Though their research indicated that they could expect a highly multicultural city, the move revealed that the area's diversity tended to be concentrated in the city rather than in the suburbs, where Monique and David planned to live.

Monique admits, "I am embarrassed to say this, but we did not look into diversity in the suburbs. We did not realize the difference until we moved here."

Coming from the metropolitan D.C. area, where the couple was used to seeing many of the cultures of the world represented in their daily lives, the two found Valencia, California, the area they eventually moved to, to be sorely lacking in minority representation.

"When we came here to Valencia, we rarely saw any minorities. The issue of diversity for us went from important to very important. We began to talk about the lack of diversity here in Valencia. How it is important to us individually, as an interracial couple, and for any children we may have in the future. So we decided to take trips to the city and to the other local suburbs. I personally noticed that the diversity in each community depended on the area. When we went to Hollywood, we did see more Hispanics and more African Americans, compared to Valencia. When we went to Beverly Hills, it was almost the same as Valencia. There is a lack of diversity in each area. It almost seems like each area is sectioned off by class and ethnicity. That is so weird to me. I am used to diversity in each area or community. We definitely did not do enough research on diversity."

The lack of diversity in their suburb not only concerns Monique personally ("Being an African American woman, the need to have other African Americans in the same community is very important to me"), but it also concerns the couple as they look to the future.

"It is an issue for my husband and myself that we live in a community where every nationality is highly represented. Our children will be biracial and will have Caucasian and African American ancestry. It is very important for our children to be in a diverse community (with many nationalities represented, not a few here and there) and also be in a community with a high percentage of both Caucasians and African Americans."

The issues are enough to make David and Monique consider relocating once again.

"The L.A. area is not meeting our expectations," says Monique, wistfully. "We realized that L.A. is a nice place to visit but not to live. We are considering moving back to D.C. because of all of these issues."

As for advice for other interracial couples planning a move, Monique says it's important to do your homework. "Do some intense research on diversity in the area that you are looking to move to. Write a list of things that are important to you, [what] you want for your new place to live. We did some research but not enough. We should have contacted organizations or the chamber of commerce to find out information on diversity in cities within the L.A. area."

8

"BEST" PLACES TO LIVE

"WHERE IS THE best place for interracial couples to live?" It's the most common question on the lips of interracial couples. But there is no definite answer. Each interracial couple must seek out their own answer.

Each year when *Money* magazine puts together its "Best Places to Live" issue, it's faced with the challenge of pleasing all of its readers with its opinions of the best cities in America—not an easy task when the notion of what is best is so subjective.

Many factors go into determining what might make a place work for one person and yet turn the stomach of another. Personal experiences play heavily in such determinations, and one negative incident can be enough to forever make a place undesirable to a person or a family who has lived there. So while the opinions of others are helpful, you must rely on your own sensibilities when forming opinions of potential places to live.

"Wouldn't it be nice if interracial couples could all move to one community and live in peace?" While that sounds nice in theory, in reality no single place can meet all the needs of any couple or family. With the benefit of polls, surveys, news stories, and the experiences of others who have gone before us, however, we are able to gain insight into a place before we make a decision to live there. The resources offered in chapter 8 detail what to look for in your searches. For example, you can look at diversity of the population, cultural events, and educational opportunities. This knowledge and your own personal preferences will help narrow down the choices of places to live.

Money magazine uses criteria such as cost of living, crime rate, weather, education, job opportunities, and health care in ranking the Best Places to Live. Unfortunately, but not surprisingly, diversity and the state of race relations are not top priorities in its survey. Since they are top priorities for you, I've taken the liberty of cross-referencing the rankings of *Money* magazine and a few other best city rankings, U. S. Census Bureau information, FBI hate crime figures, and other sources to compile profiles of the best places for interracial couples to live. The profiles have also been based, as much as possible, on the opinions and personal experiences of people (and specifically interracial couples) who live or have lived in these cities. While the list is not comprehensive, I have tried to give a fair representation of each of the selected cities based on both facts and opinions. And while no opinion of a city can please everyone, I do hope this information serves as a starting point for couples looking for an interracial utopia of their own.

Austin, Texas

Population: 656,562[1]
65.4% White, 10% Black, 3% Multiracial
Active Hate Groups: 4[2]
Hate Crimes: 11[3]
Interracial Organizations: The Community Race/Cultural Relations, [4]
    Hapa Students' Association (H.S.A.) at the University of Texas,
    Austin[5]

Although many associate Texas with ultra-conservative rednecks with gun racks and cowboy hats, this just isn't true, according to Tracey, part of an interracial couple who have lived in Austin for their entire married life.

"Austin is a liberal city as far as the people go," says Tracey. "Most people think of it as the place where cowboy hippies retire, because they can wear tie-dyed T-shirts and eat at trendy heath food restaurants without being glanced at twice. Politically, it's a conservative city—as the seat of the state capitol, it is a focal point of much of the government at the state level."

Famous for its laid-back attitude and cultural flair, it's no wonder Austin is growing by leaps and bounds (the city grew 32.8 percent from 1990 to 2000), attracting high-tech companies as well as artists, musicians, filmmakers, and students.

Home to the University of Texas as well as several other smaller learning institutions, Austin provides the diversity of a university lifestyle as well as abundant educational opportunities.

The cost of living in Austin is only slightly higher than the national average, and rent for a two-bedroom apartment in the city is approximately $955.[6]

Overall, Tracey says it depends on which area of the city you live in, but she gives Central Austin a thumbs up. "I'd say our part of town is pretty high on that list—6 or 7, or maybe even an 8," on a scale from 1 to 10.

Chicago, Illinois

Population: 2,896,016
42% White, 36.8% Black, 2.9% Multiracial
Active Hate Groups: 4
Hate Crimes: 44
Interracial Organizations: the Biracial Family Network[7] and Multiracial Families of Oak Park[8]

Hyde Park

Population: 28,630
50.4% White, 37.4% Black

Kenwood

Population: 18,178
19.6% White, 76.2% Black

Chicago's Hyde Park and Kenwood neighborhoods offer the best of city living. In a city of nearly two million, these little hamlets can provide a community feel in the big city.

With lakefront locale on Chicago's South Side, Hyde Park is well known for its diversity. It was ranked among *Money*'s "top neighborhoods" in December 2000 and was noted for its "green space, culture, and having an accessible city center."

Hyde Park's culture is unrivaled, with nearly a dozen museums and theaters including the DuSable Museum of African American History and the Oriental Institute Museum. The Black Ensemble Theatre, the Chinese Fine Arts Society, and the Ensemble Español Spanish Dance Theatre also spotlight the diversity of the community. Nestled in the heart of this community is the University of Chicago campus, which attracts a diverse community of students and cultural attractions. Yahoo! ranks the Hyde Park/Kenwood area significantly above the national average on its "Culture Index."

Kenwood, Hyde Park's sister neighborhood to the north, has undergone a recent renaissance and restoration after the exodus of middle-class blacks in the 1950s. Since then, Kenwood has become nearly synonymous with Hyde Park's booming culture and opportunity.

And don't let the numbers deceive you; those forty-four hate crimes account for the total population of Chicago. Hyde Park met *Money*'s criteria for a low-crime neighborhood.

The average rental of $920 per month for a two-bedroom apartment also includes the entire greater Chicago area, so you can expect slightly lower rental prices in the Hyde Park/Kenwood areas.

Columbia, Maryland
Population: 88,254
66.5% White, 21.5% Black, 2.8% Multiracial
Active Hate Groups: 0
Hate Crimes: 21[9]
Interracial Organizations: None

Columbia is a relatively young, planned community of about 90,000 people. The city was the brainchild of developer and philanthropist Jim Rouse. Rouse envisioned a community that would promote interaction between neighbors, encourage racial and religious harmony, preserve the natural setting of its location, and provide affordable housing for low-income families, all while minimizing the effects of urban sprawl. Rouse called his vision "The Next America" and hoped, some thirty-four years ago, to lead the way into a more racially harmonious America—starting with his own little neck of the woods.

And "woods" is right. Columbia is a rambling outdoorsy community with, according to ColumbiaMaryland.com, "5,300 acres of permanent open space, including 144 tot lots, 225 pedestrian bridges, the 40-acre Symphony Woods, 3 lakes, 19 ponds, and natural open space areas, interlaced with more than 83 miles of pathways for walking, biking, and jogging."[10]

Columbia is considered to be one of the more successful planned integrated communities and for many years boasted of having one of the largest populations of interracial marriages in the country. In years past it's been the most frequently recommended area for interracial couples seeking a comfortable place to settle down.

Of late, however, Columbia has been suffering from somewhat of a decay in the ideals set forth by its founder. Issues like "white flight" (in this case the movement of white students from a racially diverse school of the community to a new public school in a nearby community), "resegregated" housing, lagging school test scores, increasing crime, and decreasing property values in older Columbia neighborhoods have hurt Columbia.

All is not lost, though. City and county officials are looking at ways to correct Columbia's current problems and restore it to the oasis it was. Proposals to aid the city include ending transfer and open enrollment policies at local schools to promote racial and social segregation; devoting more resources to schools, especially those that serve lower-income residents to improve the quality of education; making racial integration a goal in subsidized housing; and finding a new visionary to lead the community into a brighter future.

"The best person I could describe [to lead the community] would be a person like Jim Rouse. He built this place," says Sherman Howell, vice president of the African American Coalition of Howard County. "This is it for African Americans. There's a lot of hope riding on the success of Columbia, Maryland. And being in the minority, being an African American, we want as many Columbias as we can get in this country." [11]

A two-bedroom apartment in the Columbia will set you back around $998 a month.

Minneapolis — St. Paul, Minnesota

Minneapolis
Population: 382, 618
65% White, 18% Black, 4.4% Multiracial
Active Hate Groups: 2
Hate Crimes: 30

St. Paul
Population: 287,151
67% White, 11.7% Black, 3.9% Multiracial
Active Hate Groups: 1
Hate Crimes: 2
Interracial Organizations: Multiracial Adults and Children (MAC),[12] the Multiracial Families Program at Hiawatha YMCA in Minneapolis,[13] and West Point Assembly International, an interracial church in South Minneapolis.[14]

Minneapolis is quickly making a name for itself as the place to live in the Midwest. With enough culture, entertainment, outdoor activities, and educational opportunities to please even the most discriminating resident, many folks find Minneapolis the perfect place to hang their hat. Add to the amenities the oft-spoken plus of "Minnesota nice."

The Twin Cities area is a bustling region with a slightly above-average cost of living (rent for a two-bedroom apartment in the city averages $1,018) and a promising job market. The mayor of the city, Sharon Sayles Belton, is the first African American and the first woman to serve the post. With a 60 percent approval rating in August 2001, most Minneapolis residents seem to think she's doing a fair job with their fair city. Many residents find Minneapolis an "average Joe" kind of city . . . even for interracial couples.

Paul Rosenblatt, family social science professor at the University of Minnesota, and Minneapolis interracial couple Terri Karis and Richard Powell coauthored a book on Minneapolis/St. Paul interracial couples titled *Multiracial Couples: Black and White Voices*. The trio interviewed twenty-one Twin Cities interracial couples and shared their stories. The goal of the book, according to Rosenblatt, was to "reflect the diversity of experience of all kinds of black-white couples." By and large, the experiences of Twin Cities' interracial couples seem to reflect those of interracial couples nationwide: some are painful, some hopeful, and most in line with what you'd expect any American couple to go through.

Montclair, New Jersey

Population: 793, 633

59.8% White, 32.1% Black, 3% Multiracial

Active Hate Groups: 0

Hate Crimes: 1

Interracial Organizations: Getting Interracial Families Together,[15] Swirl, Inc.,[16] 4C-Cross Cultural Couples and Children of Central NJ,[17] Jewish Multiracial Network of New York City,[18] and Inter-Racial Life of Central NJ[19]

You're probably asking yourself, "Where in the world is Montclair, New Jersey, and how did it make this list?" I asked myself the same thing when the city kept cropping up in my research. Since the most commonly mentioned places seemed to be larger cities or at least well-known ones, Montclair threw me. That is, until I started looking more closely.

An open-minded suburb of New York City, Montclair probably first gained attention as an interracial hot spot after grabbing the number one spot in *Interrace Magazine*'s 1994 Top 10 Best Places to Live for Interracial Couples or Families. Since then, it's captured the attention of newspapers such as the *Washington Post*.

Well before the days of its Top 10 fame, Montclair resident Irene Rottenberg cofounded an interracial support group called Getting Interracial Families Together (NJGIFT). Rottenberg is the divorced white mother of two teenage sons by a black father. Her organization holds meetings providing support to and sharing resource information with racially mixed families.

Another claim to fame for Montclair is psychotherapist Dr. Ursula Brown. Dr. Brown has written a book titled *The Interracial Experience: Growing Up Black/White Racially Mixed in the United States* and has a private practice in Montclair. According to the publisher, the book "interweaves research findings with interviews of children of black-white interracial unions to highlight certain psychosocial phenomenon or experiences."

Montclair counts in its favor above average-diversity, low hate-crime activity (including no active hate groups), a local university, and close proximity to all there is to see and do in the Big Apple.

At $965 a month for a two-bedroom apartment, Montclair hovers just above the national cost-of-living average.

Research Triangle Park, North Carolina (includes Raleigh, Durham, and Chapel Hill)

Raleigh

Population: 276,093
63.3% White, 27.8% Black, 1.9% Multiracial
Hate Crimes: 1
Active Hate Groups: 2
Interracial Organizations: None

Durham

Population: 187,035
45.5% White, 43.8% Black, 1.9% Multiracial
Active Hate Groups: 2
Interracial Organizations: None

Chapel Hill

Population: 48,715
77.9% White, 11.4% Black, 1.9% Multiracial
Hate Crimes: 1
Active Hate Groups: 1
Interracial Organizations: None

The Research Triangle Park (RTP) area of North Carolina is growing in popularity, both as a good place to find work and a great place to live. Known as the place to be for science and technology jobs, RTP offers countless opportunities for employment as well as education. The area is home to Duke University, North Carolina State University, the University of North Carolina at Chapel Hill, Meredith College, North Carolina Central University, the North Carolina Community College system, and Peace College; the first three of these schools have been ranked at or near the top in eight separate national "best of" listings, including those in *Business Week* and *U.S. News & World Report.*

The area's university population contributes to its racial and ethnic diversity. An appealing local job market sees many graduates staying put in the Triangle.

Upper-level education isn't the only sector of the system getting noticed. According to Magnet Schools of America, five Durham Public Magnet Schools are among forty-eight top nationally ranked schools "for novel programs, student achievement, and racial diversity."

Because growth in the area has been rapid, commuting can be a bit of a nightmare. And as more and more people flock to the area, sprawl is driving up commute times as well as property prices.

But the burgeoning community is experiencing growth in other areas, including abundant restaurants and shopping as well as cultural activities, both on the university campuses and off.

Average rental prices in the three cities ranges from $645 a month for a two-bedroom apartment in Durham to $818 for a comparable place in Chapel Hill. The same apartment in Raleigh will cost you $778, making all three cities a good value as compared with the national average.

And despite its Deep South locale, the area is as liberal as they come, according to at least one TurnLeft.com opinion: "Bottom line—this is the closest thing to a liberal utopia that you'll find in North Carolina."

Portland, Oregon
Population: 529,121
77.9% White, 6.6% Black, 4.1% Multiracial
Active Hate Groups: 1
Hate Crimes: 16
Interracial Organizations: Honor Our New Ethnic Youth (HONEY)[20]

Don't let the numbers fool you. Although it's still a predominately white city, Portland is slowly becoming a shelter for diversity, exhibiting racial growth and trends that some say are unique in the nation. With small numbers of minority communities from the suburbs, rather than traditional minority populations in the inner city, Portland provides an unusual opportunity for racial interaction.

"What's unusual about Portland is how small minority communities are," says Carl Abbott, an urban studies and planning professor at Portland State University. "What that should do is give us the opportunity to explore integration and accommodation of these groups in ways other cities have not experienced."

According to recent census data analysis by *The Oregonian* newspaper, "145 neighborhoods scored higher than 50 on the diversity index, meaning a typical resident faced better than 50-50 odds of meeting someone of a different background."[21] In addition, nearly a third of Portland children have an even better chance of seeing someone of a different background at school. Further analysis of birth records shows that one of every seven babies born in Oregon is of mixed race.

In addition to growing diversity, Portland offers a temperate climate and a bustling economy, and was rated by several polls as one of the best places to live in the United States. The cost of living is just slightly above the national average and you'll pay approximately $700 for a two-bedroom apartment in the city.

Seattle, Washington
Population: 563,374
70.1% White, 8.4% Black, 4.5% Multiracial
Active Hate Groups: 1
Hate Crimes: 7
Interracial Organizations: Interracial Family Network of Seattle-King County[22] and The MAVIN Foundation[23]

Looking to blend in? Seattle may be just the place for you. According to the 1990 U.S. census, 4 percent of the nation's interracial couples live in Washington. With almost half of all African American children in Washington's King, Pierce, and Snohomish counties born to interracial couples, the Seattle area would seem to be a model for diversity and interracial relations.[24]

"Everybody knows somebody who's mixed: a friend, a relative, a coworker, a neighbor, a grocer," says Maria P. P. Root, a professor of multiculturalism at the University of Washington and author of *The Multiracial Experience: Racial Borders as the New Frontier.*

Seattle's liberalism also makes it an ideal place for nontraditional families, according to one comment posted on TurnLeft.com. "It is a haven for liberals, with democrats for a governor and mayor. There are gay bars without vandalism, and Seattle is one of four cities with laws protecting transgenders. The area around is fabulous, and is definitely not 'redneck central.' True, there are conservative communities, as in all areas, but for the most part, it is a liberal metropolitan area."

One drawback: Seattle's cost of living is higher than the national average at 128.51,[25] and rent for a two-bedroom apartment in the city averages $789 per month.

If you're seriously considering Seattle as your destination, interracial/multiracial organizations in the area are happy to help. The Interracial Family Association of Seattle–King County offers: "If you are thinking about moving to Seattle or you are new to Seattle and are seeking an integrated neighborhood, e-mail us and we will be more than happy to provide you with a list of communities."

Another interesting tidbit: Some Seattle residents have been hosting monthly "race dinners" to get other residents talking and thinking about racial issues in the area. Sparked by the 1995 O. J. Simpson trial, the residents convene potluck-style at one another's homes to discuss the often-taboo issues surrounding race and racism. More information on these dinners and host packets are available from Seattle's Urban Enterprise Center.[26] The Urban Enterprise Center also hosts forums on race and larger dinner/discussion meetings at local venues.

There are many intangibles in measuring a city's livability—a certain smell of a town, an abundance of trees that recalls your childhood, or a feel you get from the people there. To some extent, you must go with your gut when choosing a place to call home. No matter where you live, keep in mind that there's credence in the saying, "Home is where the heart is." The best place for you to live might not have any of the qualities that I've outlined above, but if it's the place that makes you feel at home, then it's the right place for you to be.

Happy hunting!

9

INTERRACIAL RELATIONSHIPS
ABROAD

THOUGH THIS BOOK'S focus is interracial relationships in the United States, I felt it important to at least briefly address the climate surrounding interracial relationships abroad. I've heard stories of black women taking trips overseas to be "appreciated," meaning that certain countries have reputations for male populations that are particularly enamored with black females. I've also heard on many occasions that interracial couples in the United States have a more difficult time than those anywhere else in the world. I don't know how much truth there is in either of those generalizations, but I have had the good fortune to live overseas and to meet and talk with interracial couples from around the globe.

I've learned that the experiences of interracial couples outside of the United States are probably as varied as those inside the country. And while the United States does have a unique racial history that makes interracial relationships seem particularly controversial from an outsider's view, there are just as many countries without our tortured racial history whose people still suffer greatly from racial discrimination and racism.

I recently had the opportunity to talk with a Russian graduate student who is studying at Columbia University in New York. Obviously, having grown up in Moscow and then suddenly been transplanted to the heart of the Big Apple was something of a culture shock for her. A few days after she arrived, Svetlana set out to explore her new neighborhood. As it turns out, the first thing that caught her attention was an interracial couple.

"There was a couple—a tall black man, and a white woman with long blonde hair. They were standing under a shadowy maple tree, kissing passionately. Fortunately, they did not see me; I was startled and therefore shamelessly staring at them. This was the first time I'd ever witnessed an intimate interracial couple," Svetlana said. Needless to say, interracial relationships aren't common in her home country.

"Up to this day, Moscow, a metropolis of more than ten million people, remains overall an ethnically homogenous and, sadly, quite intolerant environment. 'Nigger' is the most commonly used word referring to people with black skin. Members of the large Chinese community are afraid to walk in the Moscow streets because of looking 'too different.' Two Armenian people were recently beaten to death in the downtown area by skinhead fanatics."

Svetlana explains that despite the fact that her country is ethnically diverse, decades of Communist regime caused her hometown of Moscow to be "a closed-up settlement for a Communist party–selected population" in which interracial relationships were virtually nonexistent.

However, one can't assume too much about a country's view on interracial relationships based on its politics alone. According to writer Emily Monroy, when the conservative Netherlands ruled Indonesia, the rulers "encouraged marriage between Dutch men and native women in the hope of ensuring the conquered people's loyalty to the colonizer."[1]

Since an in-depth look at interracial relationships in other countries is worthy of an entire book, here I attempt to provide a broad overview of a few countries whose overall views, attitudes, and politics on race have gained the attention of the mainstream media. The focus will be three English-speaking countries: Australia, Canada, and the United Kingdom.

This general discussion of the state of interracial relationships, diversity, and multiculturalism is for those of you who are considering a trip or a move, and for those of you who are just curious.

Australia

Recent trends toward intermarriage are dramatically changing the face of indigenous Australia, according to national census information. In today's Australia, at least 60 percent of the population consider themselves racially mixed. That may seem like an extraordinarily high number, but Australia has historically had a high rate of race mixing. The *Sydney Morning Herald* insists that although interracial relationships may be left out of the history books, "cultural diversity is written into our bloodlines."[2]

The *Herald* calls interracial marriages "one of the strongest social trends of the past 20 years" and notes a sharp increase in interracial/intercultural marriages not only among immigrants to the country, but among native-born Australians as well. Among the indigenous community, 64 percent of couples now include a non-indigenous partner, up 18 percent since 1986.

And according to demographer Charles Price, the "biggest multicultural group now forming in Australia is those making mixed marriages, creating one of the most culturally diverse generations in Australia's history."

Canada

Canada should be considered progressive when it comes to multiculturalism. In 1971, Canada became the first country in the world to adopt a multiculturalism policy. Since then, the Canadian government has worked hard to foster "a society in which people of all backgrounds feel a sense of belonging and attachment" to their country, according to their Federal Multiculturalism Program.

The secret to Canada's successes may be the idea that all residents of the country are first and foremost Canadians. Tina Hancock, who studied multiracial people in Canada, found that in all but one of her interviews with multiracial individuals, each identified him- or herself as Canadian first, "but with cultural and racial ties to other groups in society."

"Although Canada is to a large extent associated with being white, for those who were born here, the assertion of their national identity was extremely important for delineating the scope of others' perceptions and interactions with them. Part of this lies in the level of importance on which they place the perception that, although they may be racially mixed, they remain an important reality in Canada," Hancock says.

While Canada remains largely white, diversity is also on an upswing, with 31 percent of Canadians claiming ethnic heritage other than British or French in 1991.

According to one poll, 87 percent of Canadians approve of interracial marriage. In that respect, Canada might be viewed as more tolerant, if not more diverse, than its neighbor to the south. In my research for this book, each of the Canadian interracial couples I spoke with rated their Canadian city an eight or higher on a scale of one to ten for livability for interracial couples.

"The east coast of Canada is a very relaxed and tolerant place," said Jasmine, who rates her Canadian town of Ontario a nine out of ten for interracial livability. "I had no concerns about this [interracial relationship]."

The United Kingdom

The face of the British population is changing and, in many ways, more rapidly and more dramatically than the United States.

"According to the Policy Studies Institute, 40 percent of black children in the U.K. have one white parent. Half of all British-born black men and a third of their female counterparts have a white partner. One in ten ethnic minority Britons is the product of 'mixed' parents; one in twenty pre-school children in the U.K. is thought to be of mixed race," according to the *The Guardian*'s Tamsin Blanchard in her recent report on the changing face of the country.

The Guardian reports that Britain has one of the highest rates of interracial marriage in the Western world. The fourth National Survey of Ethnic Minorities in Britain found that 50 percent of Caribbean men, 30 percent of Caribbean women, and 20 percent of Indian and African men had white partners. And data suggests that British-born blacks may be five times more likely to marry whites than in the United States.

Acceptance of interracial relationships in Britain is seemingly higher than in the United States, too. In a *Guardian* poll on race, 82 percent of the respondents agreed with the following statement: "It would not bother me if a member of my family married someone from a different ethnic background." In the British media, it's not uncommon to see relationships crossing racial lines in television comedies or dramas. London couples face little opposition when walking hand-in-hand through the streets of the capital, and while acceptance does depend to some extent on geographic location, Britons as a whole seem to pay less attention to relationships that cross color lines.

"There's a history of seeing people of different shades for a long, long time," according to Herman Ousley, chairman of the Commission for Racial Equality[3] in Britain.

Multiracial issues in the Britain are also becoming discussed as commonly as they are in the United States. Following our lead, the United Kingdom's 2001 census instituted a new "mixed" racial category. The new multiracial category was chosen by some 400,000 Britons.

Diversity in the country is growing and is setting a precedent for all of Europe. Britain's nonwhite population makes up 5.5 percent (about three million) of the population as a whole. And the capital city's nonwhite population, at just shy of two million, is the largest of any European city, accounting for 27 percent of London's total population.

Yet despite its increasingly multicultural landscape and apparent acceptance of interracial relationships by the majority of Britons, Britain still struggles with many of the same race issues facing the United States. In 2000, a United Nations committee investigating the country's record on racism found disturbing evidence that ethnic minorities in the country feel increasingly vulnerable to racist attacks and harassment. The investigation also uncovered institutionalized racism among the British police. Racial tensions exist not only between black and white Britons, but among Britons of all nonwhite ethnicities, and the country is plagued by negative sentiments toward the many ethnic minorities seeking refuge on Britain's shores.

The country is taking steps to promote racial harmony and has instituted programs to assist minority Brits in gaining access to the government.

One London interracial couple interviewed for this book, Simon and Madeleine, rate their U.K. locale a seven out of ten in terms of livability for interracial couples.

"London, particularly our area, is a good place for mixed couples and mixed people. It's becoming so normal now to see mixture. The issues surface when we step outside of the M25 (the motorway that rings greater London) or into rural areas, where mixing is uncommon or nonexistent, and all people know of nonwhite culture is from the TV. Of course racism is still utterly rife and vicious in this country, but thankfully, we have yet to encounter it as a couple."

Generally speaking, interracial vacationers heading abroad should expect to simply be treated as Americans. It's probably a safe bet to plan your trip with an eye toward pleasure rather than with concerns about racial tensions.

When considering a move to another country, however, bear in mind that you're going to be there for a lot longer than a few weeks, so steer clear of the temptation to depend solely on those glossy brochures at the travel agency. Organizations like Network for Living Abroad,[4] publications like *Transitions Abroad*,[5] and Web sites like EscapeArtist.com[6] are better bets for researching an international move. They offer information about jobs, finances, taxes, real estate, immigration laws, and more—the nitty-gritty of day-to-day life in another country. The U.S. State Department is another excellent resource for U.S. citizens living or considering a move abroad. It offers an on-line before-you-go checklist at www.liveabroad.com/index.html, and warnings about potential threats abroad. Interracial expatriates can look forward to many adventures, but do your research to ensure a safe and trouble-free transition.

PART IV

GOING TO THE CHAPEL

PLANNING AN INTERRACIAL WEDDING

RECENTLY, WHEN BROWSING through the message board section of LifetimeTV.com, I was surprised to see the following annotation under the "Weddings" section: "This is the place to discuss interracial weddings."

Surprised and delighted, because it's rare to see it acknowledged that engaged interracial couples have unique needs when it comes time to plan the wedding. Sadly, many of these needs currently aren't being met by the wedding industry. According to *Bride's* magazine, the average wedding in the year 2000 cost a couple, or their parents, somewhere around $19,000. And yet, with all those hard-earned dollars being spent on weddings, interracial couples still have a hard time finding a cake topper that looks like them. It might seem like a minor inconvenience, but finding a happy plastic couple to represent the two of you on your wedding cake can be an important detail when you're planning your big day. The inattention to interracial brides and grooms doesn't end with cake toppers, however. Interracial couples have been largely ignored by much of the forty-billion-dollar wedding industry. Fortunately, the industry is beginning to equate the growing numbers of interracial couples in the United States with dollar signs and is beginning to respond in kind, with not the least benefit being little plastic couples in an array of race combinations.

Rather than stress over finding an interracial bride and groom for the top of their cake, some couples decide that fresh flowers, wedding bells, or other non-race-bearing ornaments suit them just fine. Oh, that all of the problems could be solved so easily. If you're lucky enough to have approving families, compatible religions, and similar cultures, you may find that you experience no more wedding drama than the next (same-race) couple. But add racial issues to an already hectic event planning and the story is different. It would be irresponsible or at the very least incomplete not to anticipate possibly sensitive situations.

I'm not suggesting that you plan your wedding under the laws of Murphy (though that might not be a terrible idea for any couple planning a $19,000 party), but it's always wise to prepare yourself for the possibility of land mines when you're walking through a minefield.

Weddings and marriages are a joyous time, but even wonderful things can bring stress to our lives. In fact, marriage is commonly listed among the top ten most stressful life events. When the challenge of incorporating two races or cultures into a wedding ceremony is added, your joyously stressful event can quickly become overwhelming. In fact, with widely divergent views of what a wedding should be or unsupportive families on both sides, many couples opt to forgo a big wedding and privately tie the knot in the presence of only their officiant. No matter what kind of ceremony you are hoping for, with the right resources and the right attitude, you'll be able to ameliorate the drama and ensure that you and your spouse have a wedding to remember.

YOUR ROOTS ARE SHOWING

According to Janice Murray, editor of the Ask Ginka Web site, a site devoted to personalized wedding themes, "There is a trend toward incorporating ethnic traditions into weddings as an alternative to the over-commercialization of today's ceremonies."[1] As an interracial couple, you've got the perfect excuse to buck commercialization in favor of a little ethnic flair.

Exhibiting both of your cultures on your wedding day is not only a wonderful way to celebrate the joining of your two heritages, but it also provides your friends and family members with an opportunity to understand and maybe even embrace the cultures you are joining through marriage.

How you decide to incorporate your cultures into your wedding is really up to you. There are countless ways that cultural traditions can be included in every aspect of your wedding, making the celebration of your union as unique as the two of you. Here are some ideas to get you started.

Apparel

Maybe you're of African descent and your soon-to-be spouse's ancestry lies in Scotland. The extravagant bride and groom may choose to wear traditional outfits that reflect their heritage or may ask their parents to do so as family representatives of their cultures. But if kilts and kente cloths are a little over the top for your taste, incorporating some subtler glimpses of your heritage into your wedding wear can add just the right touch of class. You can introduce such personal touches in your choice of ties, sashes, vests, or scarves in the traditional fabrics of your culture; a tartan vest for the groom or a kente cloth garter for the bride, for example.

Or perhaps even a change of dress for different segments of the day, as a statement of the merging of your cultures, might be appropriate. In some cultures, it's common for the bride to go through three to five different dresses during the course of her wedding day. Perhaps your day could include two outfits: one contemporary and one more traditional to reflect the merging of your ancestry with your own personal style. Or if you'd like to opt for contemporary wedding attire for yourselves, you might consider adorning your wedding party in some of the traditional costumes of your culture. What could be cuter than a ring bearer and a flower girl decked out in richly colored African caftans with matching head wraps to set the mood for your wedding day?

Ceremony

Considering jumping the broom or crossing sticks at your wedding? Maybe you'd like to smash a glass or carry some salt in your pocket in honor of your mate's heritage. These are just some of the common wedding customs and traditions of world cultures. If you're both American, you'll probably find that you've each come to expect many of the same wedding traditions. Indeed, wedding traditions across many cultures mirror one another. That's why adding a unique cultural distinction to your ceremony can be so memorable.

You've probably heard of the Afrocentric custom of jumping the broom at a wedding to symbolize the sweeping away of all past problems for the bride and groom. Incorporating African and African American customs into wedding ceremonies is becoming increasingly popular. One way some African Americans choose to honor their ancestors is through an African libation ceremony. This ceremony consists of a toast to the ancestral spirits and offers an opportunity to honor living members of the family by asking the elders to pass along their wisdom to the couple. In your interracial/intercultural ceremony, you might choose to combine this tradition, or other traditional African American customs such as jumping the broom or crossing sticks, with a custom of your mate's heritage. The blending of cultures in your ceremony will be symbolic not only of your union, but of the blending of the cultures that the two of you will pass along to your own descendants. The Resources section includes a few books that will help you shape your ceremony into a memorable experience.

Reception

Your reception may be the most fun place to celebrate the merging of your individual heritages. Food and music are unique to every culture, and what is a wedding reception without both? Think about developing a menu with your caterer that reflects not only your own personal favorites but also some traditional fare that represents your culture. Traditional wedding cakes vary greatly from culture to culture, so you may think of integrating cakes of both cultures into the dessert selection. Some couples select a traditional tiered cake in addition to a more ethnic groom's cake (a southern tradition) to round out the choices. Another possibility is varying the selections by course. While totally unconventional, you can offer foods from one culture for appetizers followed by a main course from the other, and so on. This will provide your guests with an opportunity to share in both of your heritages.

If you'd like to incorporate special musical selections from your respective cultures, talk with your deejay or band leader about mixing it up. For example, if the groom is Irish you can hire a traditional Irish dance troupe to entertain at the wedding in honor of the groom's heritage. Also consider choosing live musicians of one culture to perform at the ceremony and another group for the reception. If you're not sure what's considered traditional for your culture, check with your parents or grandparents, or get information from a multicultural wedding resource. A little traditional music mixed in with whatever contemporary selections you may choose can grab your guests' interest and make your reception unforgettable. (Resources for planning an interracial/intercultural wedding appear in the back of the book.)

By letting both of your roots show on your wedding day, you'll be giving your guests the best of both of your worlds and you might learn something along the way.

MIXING RELIGIONS

In addition to blending races, you may also be mixing two religions or denominations. When two religions call for differing ceremonies or customs in order to recognize the marriage as official, it may be difficult to tie the knot and still please everyone. One elementary solution to this potential stumbling block is a civil ceremony with no religious affiliation.

A civil ceremony today doesn't have to mean a trip to Vegas for a quickie wedding officiated by an Elvis impersonator. (Of course, if that is what you want, Las Vegas offers nearly as many wedding options as it does casinos, from the cheap and easy to the expensive and excessive.) Many couples find that having a civil officiant for their ceremony is the perfect way to eliminate the stress of incorporating both religions into their ceremony or of leaving one religion out all together. Civil ceremonies can include all the bells and whistles of a religious ceremony, and with civil officiants who make house calls, a trip to the courthouse isn't necessary to be pronounced husband and wife. Elaborate civil ceremonies have long been popular throughout Europe and in tropical locations that are popular among American couples seeking destination weddings. They are also becoming popular in the United States. Many traditional wedding reception locations now offer civil wedding ceremony and reception packages. Civil doesn't have to mean completely devoid of spirituality, however. "Some civil officials are willing, even happy, to include a spiritual component in the ceremony," says Joan Hawxhurst, editor of Dovetail Publishing, an interfaith organization. "Many judges and justices of the peace are themselves spiritual people, and are open to including traditions from your faiths." If you're thinking of holding a civil ceremony, you'll find many options to have the wedding you always wanted.

For some couples, though, forgoing religion at the wedding is not an option. Choosing a religious ceremony when you and your partner are of two different religions or denominations needn't be difficult, and with proper planning, the blending of religions can make your wedding unique and unforgettable. While it might be a stretch to imagine a vibrant Southern Baptist ceremony blended harmoniously with a stoic Midwestern Protestant one, interfaith ceremonies are more frequent and are raising fewer eyebrows than ever before.

The Reverends Irwin and Florence Schnurman, interfaith ministers in metropolitan New York, make it their business to ensure that mixed couples get the wedding of their dreams. They welcome couples whose own religions or ministers don't honor their religious differences. "Our Clergy strive to celebrate the union of two traditions rather than to impose conditions which the couple must satisfy," they say. They believe that the service and the content of the service belong to the couple, and they work to incorporate the couples' ideas and dreams into the ceremony. The reverends are also noticing a trend. "From our experience, there are more intermarriages than ever before. We also feel that objections to such marriages are becoming fewer."[2]

Finding the right ministers for your ceremony may be as simple as visiting your church and asking. Many reverends are more than willing to accommodate an interfaith ceremony when they see that the couple is serious about their intentions and are entering into a union with honesty and love. In fact, some religions mandate that their ministers support interfaith weddings. For example, according to Catholic law, priests are directed to help with interfaith wedding ceremonies despite any personal beliefs they may have to the contrary.[3] If you find your reverend or your partner's religious leader is unwilling to assist you in preparing the interfaith ceremony you desire, seek out other resources. Ministers who perform interfaith ceremonies recognize the increasing demand for their services, and many advertise in local papers or via Web sites that specialize in wedding planning. (See the Resources section at the end of this book for further information on interfaith ministers.)

Don't wait until the last minute to find an officiant. TheKnot.com,[4] one of the Internet's premier destinations for engaged couples, advises that couples start their wedding planning with the search for an officiant. "It can take a while to find the right officiant, so start looking right away."

Though the requirements for interfaith marriages for many religions are beginning to relax, according to TheKnot.com, there are still some restrictions you should be aware of:

- Eastern Orthodox clergy who officiate at interfaith ceremonies will only do so if the non-Orthodox partner is Christian.
- Because Islam is a patrilineal religion (passed down through the father), a Muslim man may marry a non-Muslim woman of another monotheistic faith (Christian or Jewish) without a conversion, but a Muslim woman may not marry a non-Muslim man unless he converts.
- Some rabbis who officiate interfaith weddings have strict conditions. Some will not officiate in a church or chapel, some require a commitment to establish a Jewish home and raise Jewish children, and most will not co-officiate with non-Jewish clergy.[5]

Couples who find themselves bound by strict religious rules like those mentioned above may find it necessary to consider other options to make their marriage official.

Mixed weddings may include more than one minister, more than one culture, and even more than one ceremony. The way you choose to blend your religions remains up to you and your officiants. Each couple and their officiants must be open-minded and willing to discuss all the available options.

Another option is to wed according to one religion, either yours or your partner's. You might consider this if one partner has a strong religious conviction while the other is more or less indifferent. While opting for one religion over another might seem divisive, it seems to work well if the importance of religion is much greater to one partner than the other. Be aware that, in some cases, to marry in another faith it may be necessary to attend classes to show your commitment to uphold the vows you'll take. Some religions may require conversion to the other religion in order for the marriage to be officially recognized. Check with your minister or clergy person for the requirements for interfaith marriages in your religion.

Wherever you decide to hold your wedding, be sure that both you and your partner are comfortable with the venue and that your respective families will feel at ease there as well. Bringing a conservative white family to an energetic "Hallelujah—can I get an Amen" black service can be as unnerving as taking your black family to a "stand up, kneel down, sit" white service. Talk with your partner about his or her religion and attend a service with him or her to get a feel for what to expect. Reciprocate by bringing your mate to your church. Then inform your families of the cultural differences so that they'll know what to expect. There's a good chance both will find the exposure to another culture enlightening.

While you may encounter some stumbling blocks in planning an interfaith wedding, the wedding of your dreams is possible with a little determination and planning, and a lot of love.

MIXING FAMILIES

A wedding is not only a union of two people but of two families. If your families get along well already, you and your new intended should have a happily ever after. But when there is family conflict as a result of your interracial relationship, tension between the families can make eloping an irresistible temptation. Before you throw in the towel and head for the Bahamas, consider some ways to alleviate family feuding.

Be Proactive

As you begin the wedding planning, meet with each family separately to discuss any concerns they might have. Use this time to talk with each of your folks about any potential problems. For example, if your parents know that Uncle Skeeter doesn't like the idea that his niece is marrying "that white boy," discuss whether to include Uncle Skeeter in the festivities and how to handle any questions the family might have if you don't.

As plans begin to form, invite the families out together. This will give them a chance to meet one another before the big day, eliminating any first-meeting tensions on your wedding day. It also allows you to discuss the details of the event, such as who's paying for what. Like it or not, money matters are going to be on everyone's mind, and determining who will be responsible for covering which costs will allay worries that your families may have about money. Be prepared with a detailed list of anticipated costs, what you'll be paying for as a couple, and how much you hope your parents will contribute.

If you know that one of the families won't be participating in the wedding, discuss the situation with the supportive family. Since you'll end up leaning more heavily on them, talk to them about how you're both feeling about the situation. It's normal for couples and/or their parents to feel hurt or betrayed by unsupportive family members. Getting these matters out in the open will help everyone deal with these feelings and will also help to avoid any speculation or rumor about who did what to whom. Focus on your happiness as a couple rather than on the people who choose not to support your union. While some contention is inevitable, particularly during stressful wedding planning, remember that the purpose of your wedding is to unite the two of you in love.

Be Inclusive

As your plans proceed, think of unique and special ways to include members of both families in not only the wedding itself, but in the wedding planning. People like to feel involved, so ask family members to assist with wedding details. It will mean a lot to them because it shows you value them enough to want their input on your special day.

Get input from both sets of parents for the event's guest list and seating arrangements. Their hand in this planning will be invaluable. They can help you avoid embarrassing mistakes, such as inadvertently inviting a great-aunt and her ex-husband, and can also help you sidestep potential dinner disasters by suggesting which of your relatives might have a better time seated at separate tables.

Guest list unpleasantness can be of special concern when planning an interracial wedding. Because you're probably more likely than the average couple to have guests who are unwilling to attend your ceremony, it's wise to discuss these situations with your parents ahead of time. Make decisions on whom to invite and whom to leave out based not only on your personal feelings, but your parents' suggestions as well—especially if they're footing the bill. While it's never pleasant to exclude relatives from family occasions, bear in mind that it's your special day and anyone who isn't supportive of that fact is an unwelcome addition to the celebration. If you do decide to exclude family members from the guest list, designate a representative to speak to that issue on your behalf. If the relatives are on your father's side, for example, tell Dad how you're feeling and plan together how he should respond to any other relatives who inquire about the whereabouts of Uncle Skeeter's invitation. Something as simple as "My daughter and I are truly looking forward to the celebration of her wedding day and would like to avoid any controversy. Because of Uncle Skeeter's recent comments about her choice of husband, we opted, for the sake of peace, to only include relatives who support her decision unconditionally" should do the trick.

One way of including both sets of family members in the wedding planning is to schedule a "Girls Day Out" or a "Guys-Only Afternoon." Invite all the close female relatives from both sides of the family to join you for a special spa day to get ideas for hair and makeup for your wedding day. Or bring along your mom and your soon-to-be mom-in-law to your dress fitting. Ask them for help selecting shoes or handbags so that they feel included. The mother of the groom is too often left out of the fun stuff that goes along with weddings. Make her your ally by seeking her opinion on the plans you're making.

For the guys, plan a getting-to-know you event. Invite your dad and your fiancée's dad out to shoot a few hoops or bring them along with you and your groomsmen when you choose tuxes. Afterward, take the family patriarchs out for lunch or dinner, on you. It'll be nice for your dad not to have to shell out the cash for a change. Planning these types of events will let future-in-laws get to know one another as individuals, too.

Make your special day even more special by showcasing your respective families during the ceremony. Symbolic gestures like having family representatives light the individual tapers that will be used for a unity candle make a wonderful statement about the merging of yourselves and your families. Or you might consider having a representative of each family participate in a reading during the ceremony. During the photo session following the ceremony, have a large family photo taken to include both your family and your new in-laws. Giving a copy of this photo to your parents and your spouse's parents is a nice way to say "thank you for being a part of our wedding."

❖ Vicky and Erik's Story

Unfortunately, not all interracial wedding plans end happily. But you can have a happy marriage despite a wedding disaster.

When Vicky and Erik were planning their wedding, Vicky had her sights set on an elaborate affair. "We were planning this huge church wedding, paying for it ourselves," she recalls. But despite their best-laid plans, family discontent eventually got the better of them. When Vicky's parents found out she was planning to marry a black man, they were "disgusted and disgraced." They quickly disowned her and, despite her repeated attempts to reconcile, refused contact with her for several years. Erik's parents were equally opposed to the idea of their son marrying a white woman and soon Vicky's wedding dreams dissolved. Family racism ran so deep that, according to Vicky, "there were about 30 percent who were refusing to be seen in a church with the opposite race." Rather than face that much discontent on their wedding day, the two opted to elope.

"We got frustrated with everything and ended up going to Las Vegas and getting married there," Vicky says.

Despite not having the wedding they initially planned, Vicky and Erik are happy that they avoided the tension surrounding them. They had a religious ceremony (they're both Methodist) and blending cultural traditions was "not an issue (thank goodness)."

❖ Jasmine and Lawrence's Story

When Lawrence asked Jasmine to be his bride, she couldn't have been more thrilled. The fact that he was black and she was white didn't even factor into the equation. "When I met [Lawrence], the decision was made for me. He was everything I had wanted and hadn't dared to dream about. His race wasn't a factor really."

After a relatively short engagement period, the couple wed in a nontraditional, nondenominational ceremony in their hometown. Lawrence would have been perfectly happy eloping to his native Aruba for a beach wedding, but Jasmine had other plans. So after convincing Lawrence that they should stay put, she took on the task of wedding planning, working under the theory that if you want something done right, you've got to do it yourself.

"I planned, catered, decorated, etc.—the entire wedding," she proclaims. Since neither wanted a traditional ceremony, Jasmine set out to make the day of their dreams as special and unique as possible.

"We chose a very unique setting and made it special by adding small, personal touches to everything we did. Our oldest daughter was the flower girl, my sister was the photographer, my maid of honor's husband was the deejay. We had a very special wedding."

Luckily for them, neither of their families had an issue with their interracial relationship. Lawrence's brothers and sisters are all in interracial relationships, so the road had already been paved on his side of the family. The only minor stumbling block was Jasmine's grandmother, who was concerned for any children that Jasmine and Lawrence might have. But after spending some time with Lawrence, "she realized that there was nothing to worry about." In fact their families get along better than anyone had expected.

"My all-white family got along smashingly with his all-black family. They all loved each other immediately! It was more wonderful than I had ever dreamed it could be," Jasmine beams.

Just as race wasn't a factor in the celebration of their union, neither was religion. Though Lawrence is Catholic and Jasmine is Protestant, the two decided early on that they didn't want to have a religious ceremony and opted for a nondenominational officiant to preside over their vows.

Though Lawrence's family is West Indian, because the two have both lived in Canada for most of their lives, what they'd come to expect from wedding customs didn't differ all that much. But that didn't stop them from including a nod to Lawrence's West Indian heritage at the reception. At Jasmine's request, Lawrence's mom made a traditional West Indian fruitcake for the groom's cake.

While Jasmine concedes that the wedding wasn't perfect ("My cake got lost, the wrong music was played during the ceremony, I forgot the marriage license at home"), it was perfectly unique to them. And they wouldn't have changed a thing.

PART V

RELATIONSHIPS UNDER PRESSURE

UNDER THE MAGNIFYING GLASS

MAKE NO MISTAKE—interracial couples face more pressures than same-race couples.

While other couples argue over finances, whose turn it is to do the dishes, and who left the toilet seat up, you'll argue about all those things plus heavier issues like disapproving parents, societal racism, or raising biracial kids.

Some of the pressures that interracial couples face are those of the daily variety, which you will either quickly learn to ignore or simply handle without much thought. These annoyances can be as mundane as having to reassure store clerks that yes, you are in fact together so no, you won't need to be helped separately. You'll come to simply cope with these pressures without even recognizing them as such. That's not to say that there won't be times when you feel like going off on a stranger for a cross-eyed stare or a snide remark, because the unfairness of racism angers us all from time to time. A healthy coping mechanism and a strong support system are important. The good news is that studies suggest that interracial relationships and the bonds between people in them are often stronger than same-race unions. Stronger, no doubt, because in order to survive they have to be.

Accept the fact that you and your partner will have to cope with day-to-day pressures in your relationship. As a black person, unless you've been living a supremely privileged existence, you are already aware of these stresses. Face it, though things are getting better, being black in these United States is still no cakewalk. And even if you don't obsess about the pressures of wearing your dark skin, there's a good chance that they're still taking a toll on your mental and physical health. A 1997 study by a University of Michigan researcher found that while major incidents of discrimination, such as harassment by law enforcement officers, had little effect on the overall health of the participants studied, everyday incidents of racial discrimination were positively correlated to a decline in the black participants' physical and mental health.[1] These realities, though unpleasant, are part of living as a black person; you're born with them, you can't change them, so you deal with them as best you can. For a white partner in an interracial relationship, however, entering into the realm of judgment and discrimination will be an enormous adjustment—an adjustment you both must be prepared to face.

Whether you're entering into what will be a long-term relationship or just casually dating, it's important to try to understand your partner's point of view. The shock your partner will feel the first time he or she experiences discrimination because he or she is with you is going to rattle his or her bones. Moving from being seen as an upstanding member of the community to, in some cases, being viewed as a second-class citizen may be something your mate wasn't bargaining for when he or she met you. Compassion and a willingness to communicate and learn are essential for the two of you to relate on equal ground.

SHEDDING SKIN AND UNPACKING BACKPACKS

Peggy McIntosh, associate director of the Wellesley College Center for Research on Women and author of the working paper "White Privilege and Male Privilege: A Personal Account of Coming to See Correspondences through Work in Women's Studies" (1988),[2] talks about something called "the invisible knapsack." It's McIntosh's way of describing what is commonly known as white skin privilege. *White privilege*, put simply, is the unearned rights that white people in our country possess simply because of their skin color. It includes rights like being able to walk into a store and shop without being monitored, being able to turn on the television to see your race widely represented, never being asked to speak as a representative of your race, or being able to succeed without being called a credit to your race. It is something whites grow up taking for granted and something blacks grow up extremely aware of.

When a white person chooses to enter into an interracial relationship, he or she effectively gives up many of these privileges. Sure, your white mate will see herself reflected on television much more often than minorities and she'll still have the benefit of "shopping while white," but only as long as she isn't shopping with you. As with the legendary one-drop rule, race in our country still has a lot more to do with people's perceptions of you rather than any biological or genetic data. So, while your partner will still very much be a white person, dating a black person will make him or her guilty by association in the eyes of many. You'll both soon recognize that, even when your mate isn't treated differently as a result of being with you, he or she will soon become more keenly aware of when and how you're treated differently. And because your partner cares about you, he or she will feel, possibly for the first time, the anger and frustration of being a victim of discrimination.

I've talked to many whites who have learned about race and racism via these channels. I have a white friend who is married to a black man, and she was startled when she realized that so few of the figures in her children's play toys and on television look anything like her children. A white couple who adopted a black child called me filled with rage and fear when suddenly they realized what the future looked like for their new black son. Adam Scott, a white student at the University of Colorado, thought he knew about racism until he fell in love with a black woman.

> As much as we might like to think that we are compassionate toward victims of racism (having a lot of friends who are ethnic minorities certainly made me think I was), when you're in love with one, you become acutely aware of how racism is so real. [3]

While this is probably one of the best ways for nonminorities to truly begin to understand racism and discrimination, it's a hard lesson to learn. Being a nonblack person who loves a black person quickly teaches you how to be the best ally in the struggle against racism.

While nonminorities in interracial relationships check their privileges at the door (whether they truly want to or not), the notion of shedding one's white privilege is not a new one. In fact, people like Peggy McIntosh suggest that whites willingly rid themselves of these privileges as a way of balancing the racial scales. Noel Ignatiev, author of *How the Irish Became White* and a fellow with the W. E. B. Du Bois Institute for Afro-American Research at Harvard University, calls it "New Abolitionism." He wholeheartedly favors abolishing white skin privilege, claiming that "until that task is accomplished, even partial reform will prove elusive, because white influence permeates every issue, domestic and foreign, in U.S. society." Ignatiev, also co-editor of the Race Traitor Web site (http://racetraitor.org), has been criticized for his teachings. While opponents of whiteness studies argue that white privilege does not exist, McIntosh and others contend that only by recognizing the inherent liberties that white people in our country possess can we move beyond the boundaries that still hold minorities back. Ignatiev calls those who choose to abolish their white privilege "race traitors," saying, "treason to whiteness is loyalty to humanity."

You may have heard another use for the term race traitor, in reference to those who date interracially. As McIntosh and Ignatiev contend, interracial couples should view themselves pioneers into a more diverse and racially harmonious future as they learn from one another and teach others by example. Perhaps we should learn to embrace the traitor term rather than revile it.

YOUR MOM'S IN MY BUSINESS

When pressures facing your relationship come from outside of your circle, it's generally not a big challenge to write them off as ignorance. Random haters and troublemakers can be an annoyance, but since they aren't people you care about, you'll soon forget about them. But when the pressure comes from loved ones, it can put your relationship in turmoil. Handling disapproving family members is perhaps the most difficult thing you face as an interracial couple, and when the disapproval continues throughout your relationship, it can put you and your partner under tremendous strain.

From the earliest stages of life, children ask for little more than the approval of their parents. That need for approval doesn't always go away when you become an adult. When your folks don't like your choice of colleges or aren't happy with your chosen career path, it may be difficult, but when your parents disapprove of your mate, it feels like rejection. When the people you love disapprove of your new love, you may feel forced to choose between one or the other. If this is your reality, you'll unfortunately have to learn to deal with or manage the situation.

Earlier, we discussed ways to introduce your partner to your family and what to expect when you meet your partner's family. As we move forward, we're going to assume that if both sets of families and friends approve of your relationship you've got things under control. However, if one or both of your families has irresolvable issues with your relationship, effectively managing the tension that causes will make everyone's lives easier. Here, we'll talk a bit about managing situations where a family's disapproval is ongoing throughout your relationship and dealing with the unfortunate cases when it becomes clear that severing ties with a disapproving family is the only solution to an ugly situation.

Because racist attitudes can be very deeply rooted, especially among older generations, an interracial relationship may be more than your parents or your mate's parents can handle. Racism and fear in these situations can lead to incidents of name-calling, violent arguments, and even cases where children are disowned by their parents. Anger and ugliness on the part of one's family toward your mate can breed resentment that is the seed for arguments and disagreements between you and your partner. In extreme situations like this, couples may find it impossible to continue to endure racism from within their own families. If a relationship is in constant turmoil over critical family members, couples may find separating themselves from the source of discontent is the most sensible way to allow their relationship to grow. It's ultimately up to you to decide how detrimental the problem is to your relationship and to what lengths you're willing to go to rid yourself of it.

In less extreme cases of disapproval, you may find yourself having to walk the thin line between loving your mate and loathing his or her family. Not every case of disapproval will warrant complete separation from the offending family. Political correctness has led to a quieter, gentler discrimination against couples in interracial relationships: casual remarks about "those poor confused kids" when biracial children are the focus of attention (even when they aren't your own kids); incessant "I'm just joking" remarks about—or even to—you or your partner about your race or "jungle fever"; or the silent treatment from one or more members of the family. Some couples find that though they are physically welcome into their spouse's families' homes and traditions, there is an underlying apprehension when they are around. If showing up at your in-laws' house causes conversations to cease and interactions to be edgy, you and your partner may choose to find alternate ways of interacting and nurturing that relationship.

If you or your partner is committed to maintaining a relationship with your parents, despite an underlying air of disapproval of your relationship, seek out less intense methods of relating. Moving your meetings to a neutral place, such as a restaurant, may help alleviate some of the turf tensions. Also, finding activities that remove the focus from face-to-face interaction to less focused contact may facilitate conversation and help you avoid uncomfortable silences. Going bowling or taking in a movie will allow you to put in valuable face time while keeping the mood light and nonconfrontational. Also, make an effort to look for things you may have in common with your in-laws to help you relate on a level that isn't race-related.

As a last resort, and if you simply cannot stomach faking the funk with your partner's parents or your partner is feeling likewise about your Moms and Pops, consider encouraging solo visits to your respective families. Though it's not ideal, this option may prove a suitable solution for some couples and can even be a benefit to all parties. If you can: (a) accept the fact that your partner's family doesn't fully accept you or your family doesn't fully accept your partner, no matter how wrong it may be and, (b) support your partner's wish to maintain a relationship with his or her family, then these singular visits can spare either you both from having to endure the torture, while giving you each a chance to connect with your respective families and nurture those relationships. At best, parents will soon recognize that your relationship is a healthy and important part of your lives and will come to recognize your mate as the source of your happiness.

FINDING YOUR STRENGTH

Your white partner's family is more likely to disapprove of your relationship than your black family is. In her research on interracial relationships, Christine Iijima Hall found that black families are historically more accepting of interracial relationships than families of other races.[4] Blacks may be more accepting of interracial relationships because they're more aware of how it feels to be discriminated against. Whatever the reason, there's a better chance that you and your mate will be spending more family time with your family than his or hers. It's important to support your partner in this situation.

You must bear the burden of being the strong one. That means investing in a stock of patience and understanding. It means biting your tongue when you want to shout "Racist!" at the top of your lungs. And it means swallowing your pride and being there for your partner in the name of love.

When your partner's parents don't like you because of your race, you must first accept that it's nothing personal. That may sound ridiculous but racism has nothing to do with *who* you are, but rather *what* you are. If the resounding chorus is "No child of mine is going to date a black person," chances are your significant other's parents know nothing about you other than that your skin is dark. They don't know how you treat their baby; in fact, they don't care. If they did care, they'd take the time to look at you for *who* you are.

You then face the difficult task of separating the feelings of your mate's family from the feelings of your mate. Rather than believing that your mate is spawn of the devil, celebrate the fact that something good can come from something bad. We all have the power to choose our own values, no matter what's been drummed into our heads in our formative years. It takes a strong person to stand up against everything he or she has been taught. Consider yourself lucky to have a partner who cares about you enough to do just that.

In the absence of supportive families, you need a support system separate from your relatives. While you may feel like you can live on love alone, even the best couples need a variety of friends to relate with and lean on when necessary.

Support can come in many forms and doesn't necessarily have be interracial couples groups who discuss the plight of their relationships. Anyone who loves you unconditionally and is able to look past your skin color and that of your mate is a welcome port when familial relationships are stormy. This can be a longtime friend or colleague with whom you feel comfortable talking, or even a new acquaintance who is sympathetic to your situation. Don't rule out sisters, brothers, aunts, uncles, and cousins who may support you despite your parents' disapproval. Everyone in a family isn't necessarily cut from the same cloth.

If you're seeking the support of other interracial couples, the listings in the Resources section of this book may be helpful. There are a growing number of interracial/multiracial organizations that support interracial couples and, in many cases, act in the place of unsupportive families. The key to finding a successful support system is to be proactive in your search be willing to extend yourself to those who want to help.

❖ Vicky and Erik's Story

Vicky and Erik are one of an increasing number of couples who met and fell in love on-line. Prior to this relationship, neither Vicky nor Erik had ever been in an interracial relationship. Despite their comfort with each other and their nontraditional way of meeting, both had a certain amount of trepidation about what people would think of their interracial relationship.

"We were concerned about what people were going to think, say, and do to us (me, specifically)," says Vicki, the white member of this couple. "We were concerned about our families' reactions as well."

As it turns out, they both had reason to be wary. Despite an increasing acceptance of interracial couples, Vicky and Erik were among the unlucky ones who found themselves facing disapproval from both sets of their parents.

"My family disowned me for a time," Vicky said. "They were disgusted and disgraced by me dating a black man." But why? "They really could not give me any real valid reasons as to why, just that I was a disgrace for having a relationship out of my race. I personally think that they were afraid of what their friends might think. I grew up in a predominantly white community in southern Georgia, and it was just not socially acceptable for races to mix."

Both Vicky and Erik's parents rejected the couple without taking the time to get to know them, much to the couple's dismay. And early into the relationship, Vicky had the inevitable questions about whether or not all the family drama was worth it.

"There was a time when our relationship was very new that I actually thought about leaving him just to make everyone else happy, but then I sat down and thought that me being sad and having everyone else happy was not worth it to me. I deserved to be happy and I was, so I stayed and never thought about that again!"

Vicky also had friends who weren't happy with her decision to date outside of her race. "I lost a few friends, those who just would not have an open mind and understand that the races can mix and get along."

Erik's family's reaction was just as extreme. "His family has totally disowned him and his grandchildren," according to Vicki. "They have not come around and have not talked to us in five years."

Despite all the rejection, Vicky and Erik opted to move forward with their relationship and get married. "We knew that we were in for some rough times, but thought that if we were serious, then we could make it through the storms together."

Since then, the couple has moved cross-country together and they are the proud parents of two young children. The children eventually proved to be a catalyst in resuming relationships with Vicky's family. After years of attempting to restore contact with her family via cards, letters, and gifts, the birth of her children finally turned her folks around. "I think the one thing that made the tension go away was the fact that we have two babies and they wanted to see their grandchildren. After the kids broke the ice for us, everything just fell into place."

Erik's family still hasn't been convinced, though, according to Vicky, he's resolved that things will remain that way. "Erik has not made much of an effort," she said. "He has grown to just accept the fact that his parents are not going to understand it, and he has pretty much left them alone."

He is, however, making an effort to get to know Vicky's family, despite their early and vehement rejection of him. "It was a very hard pill for Erik to swallow—after all, he had been called every name in the book by my mother. They sat down, had a long talk about their feelings [and] agreed that they probably will always have some differing opinions, but that they both love me, so they continue to work on their relationship. Since they had that talk, they have become better friends."

HANDLING DISCRIMINATION

MINORITIES FACE RACIAL discrimination in every walk of life. From subtle discrimination to institutionalized racism and beyond, learning to handle discrimination is, unfortunately, an art that we all must learn, sometimes at an early age. According to a survey by the *Washington Post*, the Henry J. Kaiser Family Foundation, and Harvard University, more than half of all black men report that they have been the victims of racial profiling by police, and more than a third of all blacks interviewed said they had been rejected for a job or failed to win a promotion because of their race. Conversely, only one out of every three whites reported facing such discriminatory practices as racial slurs, bad service, or disrespectful behavior.

Richard Morin and Michael H. Cottman are two *Washington Post* authors of a report on the survey. They write:

> Claims and counterclaims about the prevalence of racial profiling have been made for years. But there have been few reliable attempts to estimate the degree to which blacks, Latinos, and Asians believe they have been victims of the practice. And no national data exist that firmly document the pervasiveness of the practice, making it impossible to compare perceptions with actual incidence.[1]

While some have taken claims or feelings of discrimination lightly, Lawrence Bobo, a professor of African American studies and psychology at Harvard University, warns that it's not a good practice to ignore claims or feelings of discrimination.

"These feelings of victimization are not arrived at easily, or because they are pleasant feelings to hold," he says. "We have to regard them as indicators of a very real social phenomenon. For example, blacks complained for years that they were being targeted by police and were ignored. Only finally, when a cannon-load of data was shot across the bow, did people begin to say, 'Oh, yeah, I guess it's going on.' "[2]

Though you may have already learned how to handle discrimination and racism, your white partner won't have your depth of knowledge. The newness of the reality of racism will sting your new mate, and you'll be his or her first line of defense. Interracial couples face a double whammy when it comes to discrimination. While blacks and whites alone can feel relatively safe from random discrimination by the hate groups of their own races, when the races mix, discrimination can come from both sides.

There are increasing tensions within the black community on the topic of interracial relationships. Discrimination among blacks over interracial relationships is unfortunately not uncommon. Because the perception that the future of the black culture is at stake is common among blacks who disapprove of interracial relationships, debates are often heated and attacks can be downright vicious.

Members of their own race accuse black men who date interracially of wanting "trophy wives." Black women come under fire for abandoning their black brothers when they choose to date white men. Such verbal abuse or insinuations constitute one form of discrimination faced by interracial couples.

One notable attack on black men in interracial relationships occurred in 1995 at Brown University. Because they felt the lack of available black men was a direct result of interracial dating, seven black female students at the university created what they called the "Wall of

Shame" in a university dormitory. On the wall they listed the names of black male students who dated white women. The women accused these men of buying into European beauty standards that are perpetuated by the mainstream media.

You and your partner both must learn or relearn the tools necessary to handle discrimination. Learning these lessons allows you to in turn teach antiracist practices. If we all do our part ("each one teach one"), discrimination may someday become a part of the past for our children and grandchildren.

TYPES OF DISCRIMINATION

While not all of the couples interviewed for this book reported being victims of racial discrimination because of their relationship, many did mention feeling uncomfortable in certain situations. What makes one person uncomfortable might not bother another person, so many issues are subjective. For instance, stares from strangers might make you feel scrutinized and could well be a manifestation of contempt for your relationship, but they could also be an act of simple curiosity. In fact, some people report that they catch themselves looking at an interracial couple out of a genuine respect for their ability to love beyond boundaries. Don't cry wolf at every seemingly discriminatory situation, but realize that a feeling of discomfort is a good hint to take a closer look at what is happening.

Several couples specifically reported receiving poor service at restaurants. One couple I interviewed tried an experiment after having difficulty getting a table at a particular restaurant on several occasions:

> This particular time I walked in by myself, asked for a table for two, and I got a great table. When [my husband] walked in and tried to get past the maître d', they told him that he needed to have a reservation to get in. He told them that his wife was sitting already. They were highly angry!

Another couple discussed an incident at a local mall that they felt was race-related:

> Once a security guard at a mall accused us of selling stereo equipment from our van in the parking lot of the mall. I was eight months pregnant at the time and was very upset by his accusations. The way he spoke to my husband made us think it was race related but we couldn't prove it.

According to Professor Bobo, repeated incidents like these lead to the so-called middle-class black rage. As partners in an interracial relationship, you may find yourself subject to the same phenomenon.

"The steady occurrence of slights and put-downs you know in your gut are tied to race but that rarely take the form of blatant racism. No one uses the N-word. There is not a flat denial of service. It is insidious, recurrent, lesser treatment,"[3] says Bobo.

Discrimination may sometimes be difficult to positively identify. While it can occur in almost any aspect of day-to-day life, here are some of the most commonly referenced racist experiences reported by minorities:

- Receiving poor service at restaurants or stores.
- Being treated with less respect than other people.
- Being on the receiving end of disparaging comments.
- Encounters with people who are clearly frightened or suspicious of them because of their race or ethnicity.
- Racial profiling.
- Being overlooked for a promotion or a job because of their race or ethnicity.
- Workplace discrimination.

Remember that the status of your relationship should have no bearing on your situation or responsibilities in your workplace. Any employer who seems overly concerned about your spouse's or children's race should be reminded of that as well. Too often, the marital status of interracial couples precedes them because of workplace gossip and rumors ("Did you know her husband is black?" or "I hear she's married to a white guy."). Any mistreatment you receive at your place of employment because of race, whether it's yours or your partner's, should be addressed immediately. Your place of employment is one place where you should never have to defend your relationship.

HANDLING DISCRIMINATION

When you've been the victim of discrimination, you may feel helpless and hurt. Knowing exactly what to do in a racist or discriminatory situation is a challenge, especially if you've never experienced it before. You may be reluctant to report the situation out of fear that you're being overly sensitive or that you won't be taken seriously. However, taking action against discrimination is one very effective way of bringing the issue to light and helping to eliminate the practice. Taking action against an unfair system or individual will also make you feel better.

Here are some general tips on handling discrimination.

Identify the Problem

Assess the situation objectively. Consider the source of the problem and the circumstances surrounding the situation. If you feel you're being discriminated against, there's a good chance you are. If others have witnessed the situation, you may want to get an outsider's opinion of what took place. Weigh your feelings against the perceptions of others to help determine whether the situation was discrimination or possibly a misunderstanding. Go with your gut feeling; if it feels wrong, it probably is.

Confront the Offender

Talking to someone on the spot is probably the most effective way of making your case, but it can be uncomfortable if the situation is tense. If you feel too uncomfortable to address the situation face-to-face, write a letter explaining what you feel was discriminatory and how it made you feel. You might also suggest ways the offender might alter his or her behavior to prevent a repeat performance. It might sound hokey, but in many cases, discriminators may not even realize that their actions have been perceived as racist. Often, just calling the situation to the offender's attention is enough to change that person's level of consciousness and help him or her think more clearly.

If the situation warrants, such as an incident at your workplace, be sure to file a formal complaint, copying the offender and any higher-ups who may be involved. Keeping a paper trail of your complaints will help your case should the situation escalate to a point where further action needs to be taken.

If the offender is a business, such as a store or a restaurant, contact your local Better Business Bureau and file a complaint. You may find that you aren't the first person to report such an incident, which will send a red flag to the watchdog groups. Recent media reports on racist businesses practices, such as Denny's Restaurants asking blacks to pay for their food before being served, have gone a long way to ensure that businesses operate under the equal opportunity laws. If you encounter a situation that is questionable, dig deeper to find out if your suspicions are warranted.

In other situations, or when you don't know where else to turn, the American Civil Liberties Union (ACLU) is a good resource for information or to file a formal complaint. The ACLU has chapters nationwide where you can report a violation or a suspected violation of your civil liberties.

Finally, get the word out about your experience to help squash racial discrimination. By bringing attention to the situation and getting something done about it, you'll be able to help clear a path for those who follow you. Remember, discrimination and harassment are against the law, so don't feel ashamed about being the squeaky wheel.

PREVENTIVE MEASURES

An American Love Story[4] is a PBS documentary on interracial relationships that followed one couple, Bill Sims and Karen Wilson, and their two grown daughters, Cicily and Chaney, through two years of their lives. The brainchild of filmmaker Jennifer Fox, a white woman who is in an interracial relationship, *An American Love Story* gave viewers a five-part taste of what has been called the "subtle but still stabbing forms of racism"[5] that interracial couples regularly face.

One scene of the couple's life struck me as particularly relevant to the subtle discrimination interracial couples are so often forced to endure. In it Bill and Karen demonstrate a lesson that they've undoubtedly learned well in their years of marriage. Karen vetoes a stop at a small-town farmer's market after jokingly taking note of all the pickup trucks with gun racks. Though it's a stereotypical assumption to presume that pickups with gun racks spell danger for interracial couples, Karen's hesitation is indicative of the set of precautions interracial couples often take to protect themselves from certain situations. Being wary of where you stop when you're traveling or deciding which of the two of you will get out of the car at a rural rest stop are just two of the things interracial couples might learn to accept as a normal part of their lives.

While same-race couples are pulling off the interstate because someone has to use the restroom, interracial couples often opt to wait until they find a town that doesn't make them too nervous to ask for the nearest restroom. It might sound minor and it's definitely unfair, but racism is unfair. As an interracial couple, you'll learn to live these situations, and in all likelihood, soon come to take them for granted. That doesn't make it right, but until mainstream attitudes catch up with contemporary love stories, that's the way it is. You know the truth in the old saying "Love might be colorblind, but society isn't."

You'll develop a knack for protecting yourself and your family from the unfairness of racism as you move through life. In fact, you've probably learned many of the tricks already. Blacks seem almost instinctively aware of the areas of town to avoid, the subtle hints of discriminatory behavior, and negative attitudes. But while it might seem instinctive, this unspoken knowledge is actually passed down through generations of black families. Your partner, however, will be less aware of such indicators and may even be oblivious to incidents that you immediately recognize as discriminatory. When you haven't been the victim of discrimination, you aren't as likely to recognize what it looks or feels like. If something about a situation bothers you, share your experience with your partner to help him or her develop a sense of the less obvious forms of discrimination. This will benefit him or her not only as a partner in an interracial relationship, but maybe someday as a parent of a biracial child.

Jennifer Fox, who produced the PBS miniseries *An American Love Story*, says she was shocked by the realization of what racism entails. When asked to share her own experiences in an interracial relationship, Fox recalls, "I don't think I went through anything that [any other interracial couple] doesn't go through. It was really the shock of realizing what it's like to be an African American in America today—as a white person—realizing that."

LENDING SUPPORT

Supporting your mate through any racism or discrimination you may experience is an incredibly important way of nurturing your relationship. There's no need to be a hero or try to save the world from the evils of racism, but genuine support and understanding help to reiterate that you're willing to stand up for your partner when the chips are down.

Be there for your partner by validating his or her experiences. In most cases, your partner won't need you to make a bad situation better, but simply to lend an ear. In sharing the incident with you, your mate has an outlet for his or her frustration at the unfairness of the situation. Acknowledging that the situation was unfortunate or unfair and that your partner handled it well helps reassure him or her. This reassurance helps encourage your partner to act the same way should a similar incident occur in the future.

Also, stand up for your partner when he can't or won't for himself. If your partner seems too stunned or hurt to respond to an incident that needs to be addressed, step in. Again, you don't have to be a hero, but simply calling attention to the offender's actions will be enough to let the offender know it was inappropriate and let your partner know that you care enough to step in when necessary.

If your partner isn't a willing teammate in the support department, it's time to reevaluate your relationship. The mate who dismisses allegations of discrimination or informs you that they're not something he or she has to deal with isn't likely to support you in other aspects of your life. No relationship will survive such an attitude.

As partners in an interracial relationship, you each have the unique opportunity to teach tolerance to those who don't know of your relationship. White partners may find themselves in a situation where other whites exhibit racist behavior. You may find yourself in a similar situation with other blacks bad-mouthing the white race. Use your undercover activist advantage to squash this kind of talk. A comment as simple as "Excuse me, my wife is white" will make it known that such comments are not appreciated in your presence. It will usually embarrass the hell out of the offender, as well.

Standing up to the ills of society won't always be pleasant, but you don't have to make it your life's work. It isn't necessary for every interracial couple to act as activists for the cause, but it is necessary to be activists for each other. The act of building a healthy and happy interracial relationship sends a strong message to society that people of different races can get along beautifully.

PART VI

RAISING BIRACIAL/ MULTIRACIAL CHILDREN

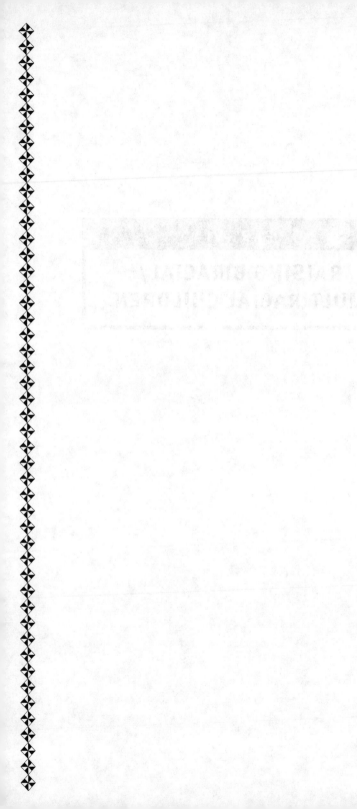

13

RAISING BIRACIAL KIDS

PEOPLE ASK ME many questions about my experiences growing up as a biracial person. Due to the common conception that mixed-race children are mixed up, many people have a sincere interest in our lives. It might seem intrusive, but people frequently ask if I was confused, if I found it difficult fitting in, if I questioned my identity, or whether I had a harder time, in general, than other kids. I don't mind these questions nearly as much as the "What are you?" ones—especially when they come from a parent (or a prospective parent) of a biracial child because, sadly, there's a serious lack of research and writing about us. In fact, you should ask questions about raising a biracial child—ask yourself, other parents of multiracial kids, and biracial adults. Whether you're already a parent or are planning to be, you're going to have a mixed-race child; whether or not he or she is mixed up depends on you.

Despite the growing numbers of multiracial people in the United States (some 6.8 million Americans claim multiracial heritages), there is a surprising lack of information on the specific needs of the multiracial population in terms of health, education, social well-being, and parenting advice. And while raising multiracial children is no different in many ways than raising any child, you will have unique questions and a special need for information because your child is the product of two cultures.

"Raising a happy, well-adjusted child is challenging under any circumstance, but sometimes, raising a bicultural child can cause worry," according to Louise George Kittaka, a mother of two biracial children and a researcher at Vanderbilt University. "Should I emphasize to my children that they have a mixed cultural background, or is it better to downplay it? What should I tell them when people point them out as looking 'different'? What should I tell them when they ask me, 'What am I?'

The answers aren't always clear. And, unfortunately, resources don't usually address the special issues facing mixed-race parents. Mainstream parenting magazines and manuals can advise you on potty training methods and tell you how to deal with temper tantrums, but the first time your child comes home crying that he or she has been called an "Oreo," you'll be hard-pressed to find solutions in the *What to Expect* books.

You also need to question your child's social and educational environments. Consider that your child will be raised and educated in a much different environment than you were. Even if your child attends the same schools you did, his or her perspective will greatly differ from yours. If you grew up in a predominantly black neighborhood, you had the luxury of being surrounded by your racial peers, most of whom experienced life as you did—as a black child. Your biracial child is much less likely to have the same reality. Not only is your child more likely to grow up in a "whiter" environment than you did, he or she is also less likely to have racial peers. Biracial children in predominantly white schools, neighborhoods, or day care centers are more likely to experience discrimination than biracial children in predominantly black environments. And even if you do your best to ensure a diverse environment for your child (probably the best case scenario), your child may still face some adversity for looking different or having a different family than his or her peers.

The reason for the lack of resources and information available to interracial couples raising children is as simple as supply not yet meeting demand. Because the number of multiracial individuals in the United States has historically been under counted or not counted at all, there is virtually no government data, statistics, or research on them. Further, some experts believe that a focus on the "problem" of raising mixed-race children, rather than on solutions, has resulted in inadequate parenting resources for interracial families. "This absence of information about what a colleague of mine calls the invisible population is a direct result of our country's preoccupation with and difficulties around the issues of race and ethnicity," says Dr. Francis Wardle, the executive director of the Center for the Study of Biracial Children and author of *Tomorrow's Children: Meeting the Needs of Multiracial and Multiethnic Children at Home, in Early Childhood Programs, and at School.*

While this might sound discouraging, there's reason to be hopeful about your multiracial child's future. There is a growing movement to organize and inform the multiracial population. With the help of the Internet, multiracial organizations and support groups are beginning to effect change in our society, from the highest levels of government down through the tightest-knit communities and families.

Dr. Wardle is the father of biracial children and is representative of this emerging trend to educate and empower the biracial population. The trend has seen parents of biracial children joining forces with adult biracial and multiracial individuals to meet the needs of a growing population.

Susan Graham, the executive director of Project RACE, is another parent who has seen the need and become involved. Graham's mixed-race son, Ryan, testified before Congress on the need for multiracial classification, and the pair have been credited with helping to add a multiracial selection to the 2000 United States Census forms.

Matt Kelly is another advocate for the multiracial population. Kelly is the twenty-something founder of the MAVIN Foundation, an organization whose mission includes increasing awareness of the multiracial population. In addition to a publishing *MAVIN*, a periodical about the mixed-race experience, Kelly's organization is working with psychologist Dr. Maria P. P. Root on a handbook that will speak to parents, teachers, and child welfare advocates about multiracial youth. According to the foundation, "mixed-race children are among the fastest growing segments entering the juvenile justice system."[1] The organization hopes that by educating those whose lives affect the lives of multiracial kids, we'll begin to see a change. The MAVIN Foundation contends that "by educating the parents and professionals who work directly with children, we will be tackling the root of the problem."

Multiracial organizations are also sprouting up on high school and college campuses around the nation. They help mixed-race youth socialize, organize, and deal with feelings of being excluded because of their unique racial or ethnic heritages. According to the MAVIN Foundation, there are currently about two dozen active multiracial organizations at high school and college campuses across the United States, and another two dozen or so organizations dedicated to transracial and/or multiracial adoptees.

While these organizations still remain fragmented, there has recently been an effort to combine efforts to draw even further attention to the issues facing multiracial individuals. Association of Multiethnic Americans (www.ameasite.org), for instance, is a confederation of local multiracial support groups looking to "educate and advocate on behalf of multiethnic individuals and families" through the local and regional organizations that are affiliated with them.

These and additional resources for parents of multiracial children are listed in the Resources section.

PROUD PARENTS

We all know at least one multiracial person: Tiger Woods, y'all! Tiger has become something of a poster child for the multiracial community, and numerous multiracial celebrities who have become household names—Halle Berry, Mariah Carey, and Lenny Kravitz, to name a few—however, your own child may be the first multiracial person with whom you'll have a personal relationship. As a result, you may have some questions about what to expect when your baby is born—and your white partner will probably be a little curious as well.

Unfortunately, there is no magical equation for determining what your biracial child will look like. Genes are mysterious things. Blacks can be born in every shade of brown in the spectrum, and biracial babies can be born looking whiter than their white parent or blacker than their black one. There is also no way to predict a biracial child's hair or eye color. A black/white biracial child may be fair-skinned, nappy-headed, and green-eyed, or dark-skinned, blond-headed, and brown-eyed, or any other combination you can imagine. The only thing you can count on is that your child will be a unique part of both you and your partner. And whether your child more closely resembles your family's or your partner's, you'll love your child more than you ever could have imagined.

GOOD AND BAD HAIR

When I was in college, a white staff member at my school approached me with a dilemma. He and his white wife were raising her biracial daughter from a previous relationship. Their daughter, who was about six at the time, was a beautiful child with a head full of nappy black hair, and my friend and his wife didn't have a clue as to what to do with it. Daily washings were wreaking havoc on their daughter and her hair. The nightly process of brushing and pulling was wearing on them all, and, in our predominantly white college town, they didn't know where to turn for help.

After pointing the couple to a local black beauty salon, my friend reported back to me that he and his wife were given the inside scoop on hairstyles, hair grease, and shampoo frequency.

You may be thinking that a story like this seems trivial in relation to heavier issues like education and racism, but a simple issue like a child's hair can trip up the most informed interracial couples. Cultural differences can present a challenge in parenting, and when it comes to black culture there's no denying that hair is a central issue. By and large, white hairstylists aren't trained, or trained well enough, to know how to care for black hair. I've come out of enough white salons looking like a deep-fried poodle to testify to this fact. Black hair is very much a "black thing"; a white parent of a child with black hair may very well not understand it.

Black folks—black women in particular—take their hair very seriously. Marketing research has shown that black women spend more of their disposable income—which they typically have less of—on their hair than any other racial group. And in fact there is something of a science to mastering African American hair. It's not knowledge that you're born with; it's passed on from black mothers to their children through hours spent pressing, combing, braiding, relaxing, setting, and cornrowing. Your white partner won't have such knowledge from his or her own culture, but will certainly have to acquire it when children come into the picture.

Since the task of family hair care falls to the female, a black woman won't have a problem with her child's black hair. A black man, though, may be faced with a situation where neither he nor his white spouse is familiar with braiding and styling black hair. While I don't know of any crash courses on African American hair, you may be lucky enough to find a supportive female relative who is willing to give you and your partner some tips on caring for your child's hair. Failing that, a trip to the local black-owned beauty salon will help you discover the right products and routines for you child's specific hair type.[2]

Identity Issues

Besides racism and discrimination, self identity is one of the biggest challenges facing biracial children. They aren't black and they aren't white, but in a society that finds it so necessary to categorize people, there will be pressure for them to choose one. In fact, "choosing one" has been the bane of many a multiracial person when it comes to filling out forms or providing personal information. Until 2000, even the U. S. Census Bureau didn't offer the opportunity for multiracial people to check more than one race on their census forms. As a result, actual numbers of multiracial people living in the United States have been unclear or based on best guesses until recently. Since the new option, of the 6.8 million Americans who reported two or more races on their census forms, 1.8 million reported black and at least one other race.

The identity of mixed-race people has been a hot issue for many years. Racist whites may fear that their race is being tainted by the notion of multiracial identification, while some blacks worry that multiracial identification will draw attention and resources away from black causes by effectively diminishing the numbers of people counted as black. These arguments are no doubt the source of the infamous "What about the kids?" question that so many interracial couples face. But we should spend less time worrying about the "what if" and more time concentrating on what we can do to provide our children with healthy racial identities.

How your kids will identify themselves should ultimately be their own decision, but it's safe to assume that their decision will be based on the information and guidance you provide them in their early years.

According to a study by the National Association for the Education of Young Children, "Children become aware of differences in gender, race, and ethnicity as early as age two." But it's not until age three that they begin to incorporate the negative messages about people who are different, so the guidance you provide should start early.

Positive role models of both races and plentiful access to both of their cultures will help instill a healthy understanding that both cultures are a part of who they are. When biracial individuals are pressured into choosing one race or the other, they often report feeling as though they're being forced to deny one parent or the other. Giving your child a good sense of belonging to both races will enable him or her to feel secure in whatever identification he or she chooses.

Another common self-identity issue facing biracial people is pressure from outside of the family to pick sides. Children can be mean and, unfortunately, will often find any reason to tease one another. Biracial kids may be seen as "not black enough" by their black peers or "too black" by their white ones. Biracial children need a high level of self-esteem to help them feel secure in the face of abuse from their peers. Providing your children with diverse surroundings (a racially diverse neighborhood, city, school, day care, and so forth) will help to reduce the possibility that their differences will be subject to teasing. Teaching your child that differences are a reason to celebrate will help him reconcile anything that may set him apart from his peers. It's also important to give your child the necessary tools to deal with prejudice and racism. (You'll find more tips to accomplish these goals in chapter 15.)

Ultimately, each child learns to embrace and celebrate each of her heritages and cultures. Whether your child chooses to identify herself as black, white, or multiracial, respect the decision she makes, be there to help along the way, and offer support for any troubles or concerns your child may have.

❖ Tracy's Story

As an interracial couple of fifteen years, Tracy and Todd know the routine. The couple met while both were serving in the military and have since gone on to live their American dream: a couple of gorgeous kids, Tracy's own business, and Todd's continuing service to his country. But it wasn't always smooth sailing for the happy couple. Shortly after the two expanded their family by one, Tracy began to feel the injustice of the world and what it meant to be in the minority.

"I remember after I had my first daughter, in 1991, driving down the street and crying when I noticed the people on billboards for the first time. First it was billboards, then it was toys in the toy store, and finally children's books. It simply broke my heart!" As a white person, Tracy had never taken much notice of the predominantly white message that society was sending. As a parent of a biracial child, she quickly became aware that racial diversity was sorely underrepresented in day-to-day life.

Tracy decided to take action—to do her part to make sure her children and their peers could see themselves (along with other members of their society) reflected in the products around them. In 2001, Tracy joined the growing numbers of interracial couples striving to make the world a better place for others like themselves by launching her own Web site, iMeltingPot.com (www.imeltingpot.com). The site is dedicated to providing a wide array of multicultural gifts and products for parents of multiracial children and everyone else interested in celebrating diversity.

"I have taken on as my responsibility—my passion—to create a place where people can get products that reflect diversity," said Tracy. "You know, no more faking the image, just simply celebrating the richness around."

After fifteen years of distance from her own family as a result of her relationship with Todd ("They still have never met him. They 'say' they would like to but have never made any real effort"), Tracy finds it somewhat therapeutic to teach others about tolerance and diversity.

"You would be amazed at how many (white) people have no clue that these products (such as multicultural artwork and home décor, greeting cards featuring interracial families and multiracial children, or multicultural children's music and videos) aren't easily obtained," she explains. "Generally people think that what I've done is not that extraordinary. People need to be educated. I have friends and family who never really looked at what they bought until they met me; some still don't. They, in essence, went along with being 'colorblind.'"

The Internet has served Tracy in other ways when it comes to her interracial family. She's an advocate of the support that can be found in cyberspace, as well as a veritable encyclopedia the resources available on interracial families, multiracial kids, and multicultural education. "The Internet has also been another wonderful resource that helps me a great deal. There are many support groups, family fun groups, e-groups, etc., that discuss everything from taking care of your children's hair to coping with rejection from family. It is a wonderful way to build friendships."

When asked to offer advice to other interracial couples, Tracy adds, "If you have family or friends who reject you because of your family, find a way to channel that energy in a positive way. While it will always be painful, know that you are fighting for the greater good."

14

MEDICAL MATTERS

ALL PARENTS ARE concerned about the health of their child. From the moment of conception, pregnant mothers focus on eating the right foods, quitting smoking, drinking enough water, and becoming experts about folic acid and other vitamins and minerals that might have been foreign to them before they found out they were pregnant. After baby is born, new moms and dads start counting feedings, hours of sleep, and bowel movements. As children grow, concerns shift to inevitable childhood illnesses and injuries. Parents do their best to comfort their kids, taking them to the best doctors, doling out the appropriate medicines, and giving a lot of TLC.

No one wants to think about the possibility of having a critically ill child, but if the situation does arise, it's important to thoroughly inform yourself about the treatment options and how to ensure the best medical care for your child.

You shouldn't assume that because your child is biracial he or she will be more susceptible to disease. In fact, to the contrary, children of mixed-race heritage are actually less likely to acquire race-specific genetic diseases than their single-race counterparts. For instance, a child who is half black and half white is only half as likely to acquire the sickle-cell trait as a child with two black parents. Further, there are no diseases endemic to the bi- or multiracial population. However, it's still a good idea to learn about any potential afflictions to ensure that you and your doctor do everything possible to screen for and, when possible, prevent these diseases.

According to Project RACE (www.projectrace.com), an organization aimed at "a multiracial classification on all school, employment, state, federal, local, census, and medical forms requiring racial data," there is "a total lack of information about health risks and trends in public health statistics for the multiracial population."

This might seem like an insignificant fact at a glance. Surely biracial people respond to medical treatment in the same way as anyone else; after all, we're all human. But, according to Project RACE, the medical needs of the biracial and multiracial population are not currently being met.

"The health care system in the United States has rendered the multiracial population 'invisible,' " says Project RACE's executive director, Susan Graham, who is the mother of biracial children.

Further, risk factors that are known to increase among certain populations have not been studied among the multiracial population. For instance, while we know there is an increased likelihood that African Americans, Mexicans, Native Americans, native Hawaiians, and some Asian Americans will develop heart disease, biracial and multiracial people's propensity for the disease isn't clear based on current clinical studies.

Some populations benefit from allies who help spread the word throughout their communities about the need to be screened for certain diseases. In the Eastern European Jewish community, involvement of its religious leaders has made screening programs for Tay Sachs—a disease that specifically affects this community—very successful.[1] However, the multiracial community remains largely disconnected in these matters. Though organizations like Project RACE and other multiracial groups scattered across the country are doing their part, their efforts can't replace an educated medical community that is proactive in serving the multiracial community.

Prescreening for certain diseases may prove ineffective if a patient's race isn't classified properly in medical records. A multiracial person misclassified as having only the race of one parent or the other runs the risk of being excluded from screenings that may detect or prevent a disease. A fair-skinned biracial child, for instance, who isn't classified as black *and* white might not be screened for sickle-cell anemia. Parents aren't physicians and can't always be aware of the potential for disease or health risks facing their children. Without the knowledge of a doctor, even the most proactive mother can't recommend that her child be screened for a disease she doesn't know exists. Proper racial classification will not only help doctors treat patients better, it can help researchers develop statistics and information about increased risk factors for certain diseases or conditions among the multiracial population.

STEM CELLS AND BONE MARROW

Stem cell research has also excluded the multiracial population and a significant portion of many races of people. When asked to comment on the racial diversity of the stem cell lines that were recently authorized by President Bush for use in continued federally funded research, a senior scientist at BresaGen Inc., one of the labs handling the research, said it was "reasonable to assume they are from white couples."

Jon Entine, a writer who has covered racial issues as they pertain to genetics, and Sally Satel feel that this is negligent. "Although this effect is surely unintended, if federally funded research is limited to the sixty-four stem cell lines approved by the Bush Administration, potential cures could end up being most useful to a narrow sliver of the world's population: whites of mostly European ancestry and some Asians. Much of the rest of the world will find that some promising therapies developed from these lines do not work very well."[2] The authors go on to point out several race-specific diseases and drug reactions that exemplify the need for a broader approach to treating a racially diverse nation of people. "Northern Europeans are more susceptible to cystic fibrosis. A specific allele (alternate form of a gene) is a potent risk factor of Alzheimer's Disease among whites but not for most blacks. Different ethnic and racial populations metabolize common drugs such as codeine, beta-blockers, and antidepressants differently. African, Mediterranean, and some Asian populations are far more likely than whites to develop a toxic reaction from Primaquine, a drug used to treat malaria and pneumonia. Genetic variants are associated with Type 1 diabetes, asthma, and thrombophilia, a bleeding disorder— as well as with sensitivity to certain foods. These are all 'racial' differences of a kind."[3]

Treatment of disease is another key matter among the multiracial community, specifically diseases that have been found to be treatable by bone marrow or stem cell transplants.

Bone marrow transplants have been used in the United States since the early 1970s to treat diseases like leukemia. Marrow transplants are a relatively simple procedure that provides a great benefit to recipients. Bone marrow must be matched to each individual, in much the same way any organ donation is examined. But because some characteristics of marrow type are unique to people of specific ancestry, bone marrow matches are often best made through people of similar racial backgrounds and makeups. The best donors for transplants are usually within one's own biological family, but experts say that more than 70 percent of patients in need are unable to find a match within their families and must seek a match from an unrelated donor. This puts the small minority of multiracial individuals in this country at a distinct disadvantage when it comes to finding a suitable donor.

What's worse, the numbers of minority donors are critically low, further decreasing the odds of finding a match for a multiracial person in need of a bone marrow transplant. According to the most recent statistics, registered multiracial bone marrow donors make up less than 2 percent of the 4.5 million total potential donors. Whites make up some 2.4 million of that total, and the remaining 1.9 million are split between blacks, Hispanics, Native Americans/Alaskans, Asians, and donors of unknown racial heritage. African Americans are less than half as likely as Caucasians to find suitable bone marrow donor matches.

Recruiting minorities to be volunteer potential donors continues to be a focus for the National Marrow Donor Program as well as Project RACE and MAVIN, another multiracial organization that works toward bettering the multiracial experience in the United States. To that end, each of these organizations sponsors bone marrow drives within minority communities and within the multiracial community.

What You Can Do

As a parent of a biracial child, rather than feeling alarmed or helpless about the medical needs of multiracial children, be proactive in educating yourself and others about these needs. By doing so, you'll not only help your child but the multiracial population as a whole. Here are some ways you can help:

Inform Yourself, Your Family, and Your Community About the Critical Needs for Minority and Multiracial Bone Marrow Donors

Joining an organization dedicated to the multiracial community helps, but if you can't do that, just the simple act of educating those around you can make a difference. Officials believe that low potential bone marrow donor numbers among minority communities are a result of lack of knowledge about the need, rather than apathy. Get the word out that the need is there and that individuals can make a difference.

Talk to Your Doctor

If you're unsure about any medical issue, speak to your family doctor or pediatrician. He or she will be able to allay any fears or concerns you have about your child's health. If your physician can't help or seems uninformed about the issues you're concerned about, find another physician.

Join a Bone Marrow Registry and Encourage Other Family Members to Do the Same

Even if you don't have a sick child, you could potentially save a life by joining a national registry. Each person has a 1 in 20,000 chance of matching a stranger. The odds may seem slim, but consider how much slimmer they are when eligible donors don't register.

Any healthy person between the ages of eighteen and fifty-nine can become a donor by following a few simple steps. First, locate a donor site or donor drive near you. Checking with your doctor, your local hospital, or even the yellow pages. At the site or drive you'll give a small sample of blood. Your blood sample will be screened to determine your tissue type, which is how you will be listed on the registry of potential donors. The typing involves determining your human leukocyte antigens (HLA), which are the protein markers on white blood cells. The tissue type is then used to determine if a donor and a recipient are a potential match. At the prescreening, you will also be required to fill out a simple health questionnaire. Once on the registry, you simply wait. If and when a potential match becomes available, the registry will contact you for further testing to determine if you are a suitable donor for the patient. If you are selected as a match for a patient, you will undergo a thorough physical exam as well as counseling or other intervention to assist you in making the decision to follow through with the donation.

Should you decide to go forward with the bone marrow donation, the procedure itself takes place under general or local anesthesia and generally only takes about forty-five minutes to an hour. About 5 percent of your bone marrow is removed, a few tablespoons at a time, through a small incision in your hip. The removed bone marrow will replace itself within a few weeks after the procedure. Most donors experience mild back pain for a few days following the surgery and some fatigue. It's worth noting that most donors say they would donate again if asked.

If You Have the Option, Consider Donating Your Child's Cord Blood at Birth

The procedure to donate cord blood isn't yet widely available, but it causes no harm to the mother or child. It is a simple matter of collecting blood from the umbilical cord after it's been clamped and cut; it takes three to seven minutes. While cord blood transplants are still rather uncommon, there is growing hope that they may help critically ill individuals. Although according to *Time* magazine columnist Christine Gorman, your own child's cord blood can't be used to save his or her own life,[4] the cells could help another of your children or a stranger's child. Even if you never have a need for the cells, the research and donation possibilities make it something to consider if the opportunity is available to you. For further information on this procedure, see the Resources section at the end of the book.

❖ Michelle Carew's Story

Michelle Carew was diagnosed in September 1995 with non-lymphocytic leukemia. Bone marrow transplantation was a suitable treatment for Michelle's disease, but because Michelle had a unique racial heritage, finding a suitable donor would prove to be challenging. Michelle's father is of West Indian and Panamanian background, while her mother is a Caucasian with a Russian-Jewish ancestry. After her father, her mother, and both of Michelle's sisters tested negative as a suitable match for donation, doctors sought out an unrelated donor from national bone marrow registries.

Michelle Carew's search for a suitable donor gained national attention when she encouraged her Baseball Hall of Famer father, Rod, to use his notoriety to increase awareness of the need for minority bone marrow donors. During the course of Michelle's illness, her father led a national awareness campaign that generated more than 70,000 calls to the National Marrow Donor Program. His efforts helped increase the NMDP's registry from 1.5 million to 2 million during the seven months of Michelle's sickness.

When it became clear that a match for Michelle was not coming soon enough, Michelle's physician, Dr. Mitchell Cairo, attempted what was in 1996 a relatively rare operation, a transplant of umbilical cord blood which he hoped would help to rebuild Michelle's immune system.

Since then, cord blood transplants have become an increasingly promising treatment for diseases like Michelle's. Cord blood has also been used to treat patients with sickle-cell anemia. Doctors say cord blood from an unrelated donor doesn't require the close tissue-type matching of bone marrow transplants, and rejection of placental cells is less severe. According to the Cord Blood Donor Foundation, "As of the year 2000, more than 2,000 cord blood transplants have been performed worldwide."

But because stem cells take longer to take hold in the bone marrow, a cord blood transplant requires a longer recovery period than a bone marrow transplant might. That was time Michelle didn't have, according to her doctor.

"We really didn't have enough time to see the fruits of that transplant," said Cairo, director of blood and bone marrow transplants at Children's Hospital of Orange County, California. Michelle's treatment, including chemotherapy, caused complications her weakened body was unable to handle. Michelle passed away on April 17, 1996, at the age of eighteen. Fortunately, her family continue their efforts to raise awareness for the urgent need for minority bone marrow donors. Additional information on becoming a registered bone marrow donor can be found in the Resources section at the end of the book.

15

GIVING THEM THE BEST
OF BOTH WORLDS

It has long been known that children who grow up in diverse families and communities are best able to accept differences in skin color as normal.

Black children tend to struggle the most with racial identity because of early conflicting messages about race. According to *Early Childhood Today* magazine, "Children of color have a profoundly difficult task when it comes to developing a positive racial identity because they receive a double message from society: All people are equal, but some people are more equal than others. If children of color are not supported in positive identity formation, they can easily incorporate racist messages unconsciously into their view of themselves and others. This negative internal thinking limits children's potential, putting the brakes on the future, cutting down on options and possibilities."[1]

Conversely, the racial identity development of white children is often completely ignored, leaving them with the impression that they are "raceless." *Early Childhood Today* pronounces this message as just as damaging as the one to children of color. "Unless we help white children keep from thinking of themselves as 'regular' and everyone else as different, they may develop a sense of distance from those they consider 'others.'"

In this respect biracial children are the luckiest. Your biracial child will benefit from living every day with at least two wonderful role models of the two races that make up who he or she is, in an environment that emphasizes not only equality among the races, but love between them as well. Unfortunately, a biracial child's home environment can also cause the child to be blindsided by racism outside of the home.

While society struggles to catch up with the racial harmony in your home, teach your children about racism and discrimination. If you encounter a racist situation with your child or find yourself witness to discrimination, use the moment to spark a discussion about the civil rights movement or slavery. Teach younger children that though sometimes people are treated differently because of their race, it's wrong. Each child becomes aware of racism and discrimination at a different time and under different circumstances. Let your child be your guide. If you have a curious child, take advantage of his or her questions to speak honestly about race. If your child seems unaffected by the races around him, allow him to discover things at his own pace, but be prepared for the discussion, should it arise unexpectedly.

Helping your child maneuver his or her way through the world is one of your most important jobs. Give your child a positive outlook, every opportunity you can, and the self-confidence to soar. Also prepare your child for the problems he or she may encounter. Biracial people are still novel enough to warrant undue—and sometimes unwanted—attention. There's a very real possibility your biracial child will have to deal with racism and discrimination, teasing, and name calling.

What do you do when your child comes home having been called a "zebra" or a "half-breed"? Though your first reaction may be to hunt down the offender and beat him or her up, hotheaded reactions won't solve the problem—and won't set a good example for your child.

Talk with your child and try to get to the bottom of the situation. Determine whether the incident was isolated or if it's part of an ongoing problem. That won't change the fact that it needs to be dealt with, but it may change how you deal with it.

To deal with common childhood teasing, licensed clinical social worker Judy Freedman, founder of EasingTheTeasing.com and author of the book *Easing the Teasing*[2], recommends talking with your child to come up with acceptable ways of handling the teasing. "Encourage children to think about what they can say or do in a teasing situation."[3] Freedman also recommends offering children nonverbal solutions such as ignoring the offenders or imagining the insults "bouncing off" an invisible defense shield. Teasing is most common among children aged six to twelve. Helping your child learn to stand up to this kind of teasing will help build his or her self-confidence.

If the discrimination is intense, violent, or clearly a violation of your child's rights or safety, step up your efforts. Again, talking with your child about the situation is the first step. Many children who are being harassed are reluctant to discuss it. Try to recall your own childhood and a time you may have been the victim of bullying or discrimination. Call on your own feelings of fear or helplessness to help communicate with your child about the issue. Explain to your child the nature of bullying and assure your child that he or she has done nothing to warrant the negative attention. Share this information from Kids Health.org:[4] "Bullies often target someone smarter, different, or more popular than themselves because they wish they could be more like that person. A bully is often jealous of the person he or she pushes around."

Next, bring the situation to the attention of your child's teacher or school administrators. Most schools employ an anti-bullying policy. If yours doesn't, request one. No child should face discrimination at school for any reason, and children who bully should be punished. Bullies often have troubles of their own that should be investigated and often don't realize the damage that they are causing their victims.

Truly severe cases of racial discrimination and/or bullying may be best handled by local law enforcement, particularly as your child gets older and as children become more aware of the results of their actions.

Finally, follow up on the situation with your child and be an advocate for her. Let her know that she isn't alone and that you'll always be there for her when she needs you. That said, try not to overstep your bounds and do allow your child to stand up for herself when she feels ready to do so.

Handling discrimination is never easy, but with a loving support system, your child will feel more secure and will be less likely to be devastated by outsider opinions.

For more resources, the Anti-Defamation League, in conjunction with Barnes and Noble, has come up with *101 Ways to Combat Prejudice* (www.adl.org/prejudice/closethebook.pdf), a downloadable pamphlet for parents, students, and teachers that outlines steps we can take in our homes, schools, churches, and workplaces.

The following are some ideas to consider for surrounding your child with a positive racial environment.

COLOR THEIR WORLD

In the earliest years of their development, research has found that children learn through play. Choose carefully what you teach your children through the toys and games you select for them. A toy box full of white playthings can create identity issues for children. When appropriate, allow your child to choose the toys he sees himself in, but don't stop there. Ensure that your child's toys reflect an array of races and cultures and carry that theme through board games and other activities.

READ IN MORE THAN BLACK AND WHITE

The same theories that apply to toys and games apply to children's reading materials. Classic fairy tales typically include a cast of white princes and princesses. Fight convention by choosing books in which the main characters reflect their own face as well as the faces your child will see in real life. (A selection of literature for multiracial children is included in the Resources section.)

WATCH COLOR TELEVISION

Most child development experts agree that kids watch too much television. That may be true, but making good decisions about the television programming your child views can help shape his or her view of the world. There has been a lot of brouhaha recently over the lack of diversity in prime-time television. Luckily, children's programming has a much better record when it comes to inclusion. Classic children's shows like *Sesame Street* have led the way for programming that truly is for every child. The best children's shows are teaching kids about good values, some skills they'll use in school, and, hopefully, how to be tolerant of differences. Top shows for diversity to consider for your child include: *Sesame Street, Arthur, Little Bill, Hey Arnold!*, and even *Barney*.

Also, keep an eye out for diversity in the videos and movies you allow your children to watch. Whitney Houston produced a wonderful multiracial version of *Cinderella* a few years ago and HBO has produced an entire series of fairy tales entitled *Happily Ever After: Fairy Tales for Every Child* that includes a racially diverse cast of cartoon characters with celebrity voices in remakes of such classics as *Rumpelstilskin, Thumbelina, Goldilocks*, and *Beauty and the Beast*.

CELEBRATE!

The holidays provide a wonderful opportunity to introduce your children to new cultures. Add a twist to the holidays you already celebrate by introducing some customs and traditions from other cultures in addition to the traditions of your own families. When I was a child, we always enjoyed learning about Czech holiday customs from my grandfather at Christmas time. Though the new traditions may seem foreign to you, children thrive on things that are new and exciting. Consider asking a neighbor of another ethnicity to participate in your holiday celebrations by sharing some traditions of his or her own. Or throw a neighborhood holiday party where each family contributes with its own holiday customs.

If you don't already celebrate Kwanzaa, consider making it a tradition in your home. The Kwanzaa principles of unity, self-determination, collective work and responsibility, cooperative economics, purpose, creativity, and faith are wonderful values to instill in your children. And the celebration is a great way to teach your child to be proud of his or her African American heritage.

In addition to adding new customs to the holidays you already celebrate, consider celebrating holidays you wouldn't otherwise commemorate. What better excuse to have a party? Buy a piñata and prepare Mexican cuisine for Cinco de Mayo. Or introduce your family to a Chinese holiday by celebrating Chinese New Year. Use the Internet to look for ideas about how to celebrate holidays that are foreign to you. Many card shops carry calendars that include dates of holidays from around the world.

Choose Educational Opportunities

When possible, choose a neighborhood and school that are as diverse as possible for your children. Surrounding your child with a wide array of children of differing cultures, races, and ethnicities will reinforce the knowledge that differences are worthy of celebrating and will help your child build healthy relationships with many different people.

Beyond diversity among the children at school or day care, it helps to have diversity among school staff as well. Diversity among the staff will help ensure that the curriculum involves the races of all the children in the school.

Be active in your child's education. Consider joining the PTA or volunteering at your child's school to help you get a true feel for your child's school. Ensure that you're satisfied with the quality of education—both multicultural and otherwise—that your child is receiving.

LEAD BY EXAMPLE

Positive role models are the best way to lead your children into a positive future. Kids love to emulate their parents, so set a good example by practicing what you preach. Let your children know that racism and intolerance aren't inevitable. Give them the words to use to speak out against racism and discrimination and make it a practice to do so yourself. Show them how to accept differences by accepting them yourself.

Children are naturally curious about differences. And while sometimes that curiosity can be embarrassing, particularly if you find your child staring, pointing, or talking loudly about someone's differences, it's important not to stifle his or her curiosity and to explain that differences are beautiful. Rather than hushing your child in these instances, make it a point to explain the differences on the spot and show your child that though people are different from his or her, it doesn't make them bad or inferior.

FOSTER FRIENDSHIPS

Encourage your child to form friendships with children of other races. At early ages, while kids will recognize differences in skin color, they will not have learned to equate those differences with racism or discrimination. Enabling your child to meet and spend time with children of other races will help affirm that skin color doesn't make any difference in how people should be treated. If you've managed to find a racially and ethnically diverse school or day care for your child, these friendships will likely occur naturally and you'll only be left to provide the snacks and sleepover opportunities. Getting to know the parents of your child's playmates helps, too, so extend yourself to others and foster friendships of your own to reinforce your child's attempts.

BEAT DOWN STEREOTYPES

Just as it can be a challenge to avoid gender stereotyping your child, avoiding racial stereotypes is a problem as well. Stereotypes are so prevalent in our society that sometimes we don't even realize we've subscribed to them. Make a conscious effort to not allow negative stereotyping in your home and set the example for your child. The same holds true for positive stereotypes. Stereotypes such as all blacks are good athletes or all Asians are good at math are just as destructive as the negative ones because they are based on race rather than individual ability.

By paying attention to the messages that we—and society—send to our biracial children we can raise them to be healthy, well-adjusted individuals who understand that our differences are what make us beautiful. Good parenting requires a little bit of common sense and a lot of love, and fortunately for us, love is the easy part.

CONCLUSION

INTERRACIAL COUPLES ARE just like any other couple in many ways—we meet, we fall in love, and we break up. We laugh, we weep. We marry, we divorce. We have children together, we grow old. And we do all this with no more consistency and no fewer guarantees than couples we're told are more the norm. What *does* make interracial couples unique is the fact that to so many others (and sometimes even to ourselves), the very existence of interracial relationships challenges the conventional wisdom that we seek out those who are like us. We challenge the notion that the races are so fundamentally and/or culturally different that they can't possibly be compatible on an interpersonal level. The trouble with that thinking is that "like us" and "compatible" are terms that cannot be defined by race.

Interracial couples take a great deal of pride in their relationships and their families, and rightfully so. We stand as examples that the racial barriers society has constructed don't have to divide us. We set the standard for racial harmony and we provide loving reminders that there is hope for healing.

Stepping out into an interracial relationship is the beginning of a rich and wonderful adventure. Wherever you're at on your voyage, I wish you a happy journey.

RESOURCES

❖ Biracial/Multiracial Organizations

These organizations assist biracial/multiracial individuals such as the children of interracial couples.

Association of Multiethnic Americans
5215 N. Sabino Canyon Road
Tucson, AZ 85750
(877) 954-AMEA
www.ameasite.org
info@AMEAsite.org
The Association of Multiethnic Americans is an umbrella group of organizations that educate and advocate on behalf of the multiethnic population. The bulk of the group's activities occur at the affiliate level, with local affiliates in several cities across the United States and Canada. Its Web site provides contact information for its current affiliates as well as information on forming a local affiliate.

Center for the Study of Biracial Children
c/o Francis Wardle, Ph.D.

2300 S. Krameria Street
Denver, CO 80222
(303) 692-9008
www.csbc.cncfamily.com
The Center for the Study of Biracial Children is a Web-based organization offering information, education, and support to interracial families and multiracial/multiethnic individuals. The organization is under the direction of Dr. Francis Wardle, who is a father of biracial children.

Interracial Voice
P.O. Box 560185
College Point, NY 11356-0185
(212) 539-3872 (voicemail)
www.webcom.com/~intvoice
intvoice@webcom.com
Interracial Voice is the brainchild of Charles Michael Byrd, a mixed-race activist. Interracial Voice is an independent Web-based publication that advocates the recognition of mixed-race people as a unique and separate racial entity. The publication offers opinion pieces and commentary relevant to the mixed-race experience as well as reviews, research assistance, and additional resources.

MASC (Multiracial Americans of Southern California)
12228 Venice Boulevard, #452
Los Angeles, CA 90066
(310) 836-1535
www.multiculti.org
MASC is a nonprofit organization addressing the social, cultural, and educational interests of multiracial and multicultural individuals, couples, and families through social interaction, discussion groups, and conferences. MASC is a charter member of the Association of Multiethnic Americans.

The MAVIN Foundation
600 First Avenue, Suite 501
Seattle, WA 98104
(206) 622-7101
(206) 622-2231 (fax)
www.mavinfoundation.org
info@mavinfoundation.org
The MAVIN Foundation is a nonprofit organization working to increase awareness of multiracial individuals and the unique issues facing this segment of the population. It aims to accomplish this mission through unique community projects and events, educational publications, and collaboration with other organizations and corporations.

Multiethnics of Southern Arizona in Celebration (MOSAIC)
P.O. Box 64236
Tucson, AZ 85728-4236
(520) 615-2029
(520) 323-6819 (fax)
MOSAIC is an affiliate of the Association of Multiethnic Americans. It holds monthly meetings and publishes a newsletter for its members, which include multiracial and multiethnic couples and families.

The Multiracial Activist
P.O. Box 8208
Alexandria, VA 22306-8208
(760) 875-8547 (also the fax number)
www.multiracial.com
editor@multiracial.com
The Multiracial Activist is an on-line activist site and journal advocating for mixed-race individuals as well as interracial couples and families. The site offers articles, commentary, and resources for those who advocate ending racial classification.

National Association for Multicultural Education (NAME)
733 15th Street NW, Suite 430
Washington, DC 20005
(202) 628-6263
www.nameorg.org
NAME advocates educational equality by bringing together individuals and groups interested in multicultural education from all levels of the education system. NAME has chapters in twenty-two states and represents educators from preschool through higher education.

Project RACE
2910 Kerry Forest Parkway, D4-129
Tallahassee, FL 32309
(850) 894-8540 (fax)
www.projectrace.com
projrace@aol.com
Project RACE is a national nonprofit organization at the head of the movement for multiracial classification. Project RACE advocates multiracial classification on all school, employment, state, federal, local, census, and medical forms. Membership in the organization is free and is available through its Web site.

Swirl
16 West 32nd Street, Suite 10A
New York, NY 10001
(212) 561-1773
www.swirlinc.org
jenchau@swirlinc.org
Swirl aims to unite the New York–area mixed-race community by offering support to individuals for all aspects of the mixed-race experience: mixed families, mixed individuals, transracial adoptees, and interracial/cultural couples. The group hopes to accomplish this mis-

sion through several events each month, both social and organizational, and via its on-line discussion group.

❖ Interracial Couple and Family Organizations

**4C (Cross Cultural Couples & Children) of Plainsboro,
New Jersey**
P.O. Box 8
Plainsboro, N.J. 08536
(609) 448-8823
LEdwards4C@aol.com
An organization for New Jersey area interracial couples and their children founded by Lisa and Kelly Giblin. 4C provides social interaction and support to local interracial families.

Biracial Family Network (BFN)
Box 3214
Chicago, IL 60654-0214
(773) 288-3644
www.ameasite.org/bfn.asp
The Biracial Family Network, founded in 1980, is a Chicago-based affiliate of the Association of Multiethnic Americans providing support for biological and adoptive multiracial and multiethnic families.

G.I.F.T. (Getting Interracial Families Together)
P.O. Box 1281
Montclair, NJ 07042
(973) 783-0083
(973) 783-4407 (fax)
www.njgift.org
NJGIFT@aol.com

Getting Interracial Families Together is a Montclair, New Jersey–based group bringing interracial/intercultural families together for social activities and support. G.I.F.T schedules social outings for its members an provides an e-mail newsletter.

GIFT
103 Green Lake Drive
Greenville, NC 29607
(864) 233-4872
speclink@greenville.infi.net
GIFT is a sub-group of Special Link, a national adoption linking network that seeks to find adoptive families for black or biracial infants and children. GIFT brings interracial families together for sharing and support and to help biracial children encounter and form friendships with other families similar to their own.

Honor Our New Ethnic Youth (HONEY), Eugene, Oregon
P.O. Box 23241
Eugene, OR 97402
(541) 343-4023
EugeneHoney@aol.com
HONEY, an affiliate of the Association of Multiethnic Americans, is a Eugene, Oregon–based group focusing on the cultural needs of local children. The group sponsors a Saturday Culture Club for kids and works with the Oregon Council on Multiracial Affairs in Portland on annual events.

International Interracial Association
www.i3n.net
konrad@pobox.com
The International Interracial Association is a Web-based organization aimed at "promoting interracial and intercultural harmony worldwide." Via its Web site, you can access links to additional interracial

resources, a discussion forum, and a calendar of worldwide events of interest to the interracial community.

Interracial Club of Buffalo
Box 400 (Amherst Branch)
Buffalo, NY 14226
(716) 875-6958
medwo32688@aol.com
The Interracial Club of Buffalo offers community and social activities for Buffalo-area interracial families and couples. Membership includes a club newsletter that highlights information and resources pertinent to interracial families. The club also sponsors periodic guest speakers to lecture on topics of interest to the community.

Inter-racial Families in Fellowship, Ohio
Columbus, Ohio/Central area
(614) 447-1586
janet@simplyliving.org
www.simplyliving.org/ifif/
Delaware, Ohio/Northern area
wolftale@wolftale.net

Newark, Ohio/Eastern area
(740) 366-4967
alexnan@alltel.net

Inter-racial Families in Fellowship is a Columbus, Ohio–based community of interracial families who come together for fellowship, play groups, and support. The group welcomes all interracial/multiracial families, whether by adoption or by marriage and adoption.

The Interracial Family Circle
Box 53291
Washington, DC 20009

(202) 393-7866 or (800) 500-9040 (voice mail)
www.geocities.com/Heartland/Estates/4496
ifcweb@yahoo.com
The Interracial Family Circle is a D.C.-area group that provides community for multiracial families, couples, and individuals. The group holds social gatherings for its members (there are membership dues) and also offers a newsletter that is available to members and, for a fee, to those outside of the D.C. metro area.

Interracial Family Network of Seattle-King County
16541 Redmond Way, Suite 105
Redmond, WA 98052-4482
ifns@isomedia.com
www.isomedia.com/homes/duncan/interracial.html
The Interracial Family Network of Seattle-King County aims to provide networking options for interracial families in its local region. The group offers social events, support, and information about the local area via its Web site for interracial families considering a relocation.

Jewish Multiracial Network
307 Seventh Avenue, Suite 900
New York, NY 10001
(212) 242-5598
www.multiracialjewishnet.org
info@jmnetwork.org
The Jewish Multiracial Network exists to bring Jewish multiracial families together to learn about and celebrate their Judaism.

New England Alliance of Multiracial Families (NEAMF)
P.O. Box 833
Natick, MA 01760
(617) 965-3287

www.neamf.org

info@neamf.org

NEAMF's goal is to help people celebrate their diversity. The organization is a nonprofit, volunteer-run group of multiracial families of all backgrounds and circumstances. For an annual membership fee, the organization offers social events, children's programs, and a newsletter.

Urban Enterprise Center

1301 Fifth Avenue, Suite 2400

Seattle, WA 98101

(206) 389-7337

www2.seattlechamber.com/uec/initiatives/race.htm

lynnc@seattlechamber.com

Seattle's Urban Enterprise Center is the organization responsible for the innovative race dinners, dinner meetings where local residents are encouraged to openly discuss racial issues. The organization also hosts guest speakers and youth forums to get teens involved in the dialogue.

✤ Interracial Fiction

Briscoe, Edward G. *Marble Cake*. San Jose, CA: iUniverse.com, 2000.

Cross, Kathleen. *Skin Deep*. New York: Avon Romance, 1999.

Cross, Kathleen. *White Chocolate*. New York: Forge Books, 1999.

Dickey, Jerome. *Milk in My Coffee*. New York: Signet, 1999.

Kitt, Sandra. *Color of Love*. New York: Signet, 1995.

Sanders, Dori. *Clover*. New York: Fawcett Books, 1994.

Walker, Alice. *The Way Forward Is with a Broken Heart*. New York: Ballantine Books, 2001.

West, Dorothy. *The Wedding*. New York: Anchor, 1996.

❖ Interracial Films

Guess Who's Coming to Dinner, Columbia, 1967
Katharine Houghton and Sidney Poitier play the couple in this classic interracial romance. When a proper white gal brings home a black man in 1960s America you know all hell will break loose, even if he is Sidney Poitier. (Coincidentally, Poitier is interracially married in real life to actress Joanna Shimkus.)

Jungle Fever, Universal, 1991
Wesley Snipes and Annabella Sciorra star in this interracial romance that had everyone singing, "He's got jungle fever, she's got jungle fever." Snipes plays Flipper Purify, a successful married architect who finds himself in a torrid love affair with Sciorra's Angie Tucci that causes his marriage to crumble and makes both question the complexities of their relationship.

Mission: Impossible 2, Paramount, 2000
Tom Cruise and Thandie Newton pair up as the interracial couple in this sequel film. The interracial romance isn't the theme of this action film, but just the fact that race isn't an issue in this case makes it worth mentioning. (Thandie Newton is a biracial British actress who is interracially married to British screenwriter Oliver Parker.)

Mississippi Masala, Samuel Goldwyn, 1992
In this film, Denzel Washington plays Demetrius, a young black entrepreneur who falls in love with Mina, an Indian woman portrayed by Sarita Choudhury.

Monster's Ball, Lions Gate Films, 2001
This movie helped Halle Berry make history, earning her the Best Actress Academy Award. Berry stars with Billy Bob Thornton as Leticia and Hank, an unlikely interracial pair who spark a fiery romance. She comes to find out he was involved in her husband's execution. A

gritty movie. (Halle Berry is the biracial daughter of a white mother and a black father.)

O, Lions Gate Films, 2001
Julia Stiles (Desi) has an interracial romance with Mehki Phifer (Odin) in this updated spin on Shakespeare's *The Tragedy of Othello*.

Othello, Columbia, 1995
You might call William Shakespeare ahead of his time. The interracial romance between his Othello and Desdemona is played out on the big screen by Laurence Fishburne and Irene Jacob.

Save the Last Dance, Paramount, 2001
Julia Stiles and Sean Patrick Thomas star as an unlikely teenaged interracial couple in this critically panned, somewhat too-good-to-be-true hip-hop film.

Swordfish, Warner Bros., 2001
Swordfish might best be known for Halle Berry's gratuitous nude scene, but it's also worth mentioning that Berry plays the love interest of top spy John Travolta in this cyber-flick.

White Nights, 1986
Gregory Hines, Mikhail Baryshnikov, and Isabella Rosselini star in this very fine dance movie that features Hines and Rosselini in an interracial relationship in Russia. Hines defects there due to his anger about American racism and the Vietnam War.

✤ Medical Resources

American Red Cross
National Cord Blood Program
3131 N. Vancouver Avenue

Portland, OR 97227
(503) 284-1234 ext. 709
(503) 528-1711 (fax)

Cord Blood Donor Foundation
1200 Bayhill Drive, Suite 301
San Bruno, CA 94066
(650) 635-1452
(650) 635-1428 (fax)
www.cordblooddonor.org

National Marrow Donor Program
3001 Broadway Street Northeast, Suite 500
Minneapolis, MN 55413-1753
General information: (800) MARROW2 [(800) 627-7692]
The Office of Patient Advocacy (OPA): (888) 999-6743
www.marrow.org

❖ Multicultural Products

iMeltingPot
iMeltingPot.com, LLC
4045 NW 64th Street, Suite 104
Oklahoma City, OK 73116
(405) 608-1110
(775) 822-6480 (fax)
www.imeltingpot.com
info@imeltingpot.com
iMeltingPot.com has a large and well-rounded selection of multicultural products and gifts including apparel, jewelry, stationery, and home decor. The Web site also includes links to resources for racially, culturally, or otherwise diverse families.

Interracial Club of Buffalo Products
Box 400 (Amherst Branch)
Buffalo, NY 14226
(716) 875-6958
medwo32688@aol.com
www.folksites.com/interracial-club
The Interracial Club of Buffalo Products sells interracial and multicultural items by mail order. The organization also publishes a
bimonthly newsletter with items of interest to the interracial/multi-
cultural community.

Multicultural Kids
P.O. Box 757
Palatine, IL 60078-0757
(847) 991-2919 (also the fax number)
(800) 711-2321
www.multiculturalkids.com
Multicultural Kids is an on-line store offering books, games, arts
and crafts, dolls, and musical products for today's preschool and
elementary-age child. Multicultural Kids aims to increase children's
knowledge of themselves, foster self-esteem, and teach tolerance.

✤ Raising Biracial Children

Books for Raising Children

Funderburg, Lise. *Black, White, Other: Biracial Americans Talk
    About Race and Identity.* New York: William Morrow and
    Company, 1994.
Gaskins, Pearl Fuyo, editor. *What Are You?: Voices of Mixed-Race
    Young People.* New York: Henry Holt, 1999.

Gibel Azoulay, Katya. *Black, Jewish, and Interracial: It's Not the Color of Your Skin, but the Race of Your Kin*. Durham, NC: Duke University Press, 1997.

Kaeser, Gigi, photographer, et al. *Of Many Colors: Portraits of Multiracial Families*. Amherst, MA: University of Massachusetts Press, 1997.

Lazarre, Jane. *Beyond the Whiteness of Whiteness: Memoir of a White Mother of Black Sons*. Durham, NC: Duke University Press, 1996.

Nash, Gary B. *Forbidden Love: The Secret History of Mixed Race America*. New York: Henry Holt, 1999.

O'Hearn, Claudine C. *Half and Half: Writers on Growing Up Biracial and Bicultural*. New York: Pantheon Books, 1998.

Thomas, Rebecca L. *Connecting Cultures: A Guide to Multicultural Literature for Children*. Westport, CT: Bowker-Greenwood Imprint, 1996.

Walker, Rebecca. *Black, White, and Jewish: Autobiography of a Shifting Self*. New York: Riverhead Books, 2000.

Wardle, Francis, Dr. *Tomorrow's Children: Meeting the Needs of Multiracial and Multiethnic Children at Home, in Early Childhood Programs, and at School*. Denver, CO: Center for the Study of Biracial Children, 1999.

Wright, Marguerite A. *I'm Chocolate, You're Vanilla: Raising Healthy Black and Biracial Children in a Race-Conscious World*. San Francisco, CA: Jossey-Bass, 1998.

Multicultural Books for Children

Adoff, Arnold, et al. *Black Is Brown Is Tan*. New York: Harper Collins, 1992.

Cisneros, Sandra. *Hairs/Pelitos*. New York: Random House, 1997.

Davol, Marguerite W., et al. *Black, White, Just Right*. Morton Grove, IL: Albert Whitman and Company, 1993.

Hamanaka, Sheila. *All the Colors of the Earth*. New York: William Morrow and Company, 1994.

Igus, Toyomi. *Two Mrs. Gibsons*. San Francisco, CA: Childrens Book Press, 2001.

Kandel, Bethany. *Trevor's Story: Growing Up Biracial*. Minneapolis, MN: Lerner Publications Company, 1997.

Kates, Bobbi Jane. *We're Different, We're the Same*. New York: Random House, 1992.

Katz , Karen. *The Colors of Us*. Austin, TX: Holt Rinehart and Winston, 1999.

Kissinger, Katie. *All the Colors We Are: The Story of How We Get Our Skin Color*. St. Paul, MN: Redleaf Press, 1997.

Machado, Ana Maria. *Nina Bonita*. La Jolla, CA: Kane/Miller Book Publishers, 1996.

McNamee, Graham. *Nothing Wrong with a Three-Legged Dog*. New York: Delacorte Press, 2000.

Rattigan, Jama Kim. *Dumpling Soup*. New York: Little Brown and Company, 1993.

Richardson, Judith Benet. *First Came the Owl*. New York: Henry Holt, 1996.

Simon, Norma, et al. *Why Am I Different?* Morton Grove, IL: Albert Whitman and Company, 1993.

Williams, Vera B. *More, More, More, Said the Baby: Three Love Stories*. New York: Greenwillow, 1990.

Wing, Natasha, et al. *Jalapeño Bagels*. New York: Atheneum, 1996.

Woodson, Jacqueline. *From the Notebooks of Melanin Sun*. New York: Scholastic Trade, 1995.

✤ Wedding Resources

Books

Roney, Carley. *The Knot Guide to Wedding Vows and Traditions: Readings, Rituals, Music, Dances, Speeches, and Toasts*. New York: Broadway Books, 2000.

Spangenberg, Lisl M. *Timeless Traditions: A Couple's Guide to Wedding Customs Around the World.* New York: Universe Publishing, 2001.

Stewart, Arlene Hamilton. *A Bride's Book of Wedding Traditions.* New York: Hearst Books, 1995.

Officiants

The Ark Interfaith Services
3 Turnberry Court
Middle Island, NY 11953
(631) 924-0038
www.arkinterfaith.com/index.htm
rmgrace@optonline.net
The Ark Interfaith Services is a New York–based ministry that offers interfaith wedding services and premarital counseling to interfaith couples. The Ark honors "all faiths and philosophies of the world" to ensure couples have the wedding of their dreams.

Ask Ginka
www.AskGinka.com
ginka@askginka.com
Ask Ginka offers wedding advice, information on different cultural wedding traditions, and lists of additional resources for planning a cross-cultural wedding.

Cantor Ellie Shaffer
www.InterfaithWedding.com
ellie@interfaithwedding.com
Cantor Ellie Shaffer specializes in Jewish/Christian interfaith weddings in Pennsylvania, New Jersey, and Delaware.

Interfaith Wedding Services
The Reverends Ernest and Florence Schnurman
(631) 345-3606
www.weddingclergy.com
weddings@alphamedia.net
The Reverends Schnurman are interfaith ministers who welcome marrying couples in the New York/Long Island area whose own religions choose not to honor their religious differences.

Rabbi Laurence Aryeh Alpern
(518) 893-0808
www.rabbiweddings.com
RabbiAlpern@aol.com
Rabbi Alpern will travel anywhere in the world to co-officiate a Jewish/Christian interfaith wedding.

Wedding Accessories

Blind Heart
PMB 109
1148 Pulaski Highway, Suite 107
Bear, DE 19701-1306
Toll-Free: (866) 326-1816
In Delaware: (302) 326-1816
(302) 326-0206 (fax)
www.blindheart.com
customerservice@blindheart.com
Blind Heart provides custom wedding caketops (with interracial brides and grooms), ethnic wedding favors, and wedding accessories from several cultures.

NOTES

Chapter 1: Meeting Your Match

1 "Findings for Research on Interracial Marriage." *Interrace Magazine* 7:16, 1997.

Chapter 2: Making the Commitment

1 The Implicit Association Tests are available on-line at www.tolerance.org/hidden_bias/index.html. If you're curious about uncovering your own hidden biases about race, skin tone, age, or gender, consider yourself forewarned—according to the site, "Your test results may disturb you."

2 www.tolerance.org/hidden_bias/index.html.

3 www.matchscene.com

4 www.tolerance.org/hidden_bias/tutorials/04.html.

Chapter 3: Facts and Fallacies

1 Mkhondo, Rich. "Love Changes U.S. Racial Landscape." *Cape Argus*, August 13, 1997. Distributed via *Africa News Online* (accessed via www.sistahspace.com/nommo/ir10.html).

2 Chideya, Farai. *Don't Believe the Hype: Fighting Cultural Misinformation About African-Americans*, New York, Plume/Penguin (1995), p. 4.

3 Swanbrow, D. "Intimate relationships between races more common than thought." *University of Michigan News and Information Service* (2000). www.umich.edu/~newsinfo/Releases/2000/Mar00/r032300a.html (accessed 11/26/01).

4 Besharov, Douglas J., and Sullivan, Timothy S. "One Flesh: America Is Experiencing an Unprecedented Increase in Black-White Intermarriage." *New Democrat*, July–August 1996, p. 19.

5   Griffith, S. "Churches see increasing acceptance of interracial marriage." *Baptist Standard*, January 5, 2000. www.baptiststandard.com/2000/1_5/pages/interracial.html (accessed 11/27/01).

6   Besharov and Sullivan.

7   Greico, E. M., and Cassidy, R. C. *U.S. Census Bureau's Overview of Race and Hispanic Origin 2000* (2000). www.census.gov/prod/2001pubs/c2kbr01-1.pdf (accessed 11/26/01).

8   Suro, Roberto. "Mixed Doubles," *American Demographics*, November 1999, pp. 58–59.

Chapter 4: Extra Extraordinary Couples

1   Pierce, T. "Who Needs It." *Blacklight*, February 2001. www.blacklightonline.com/who needs.html (accessed 11/29/01).

2   www.blacklightonline.com.

3   Carter, C. "I Know Who I Am." *Blacklight*, February 2001. www.blacklightonline.com/iknow.html (accessed 11/29/01).

4   Swanbrow, D. "Intimate relationships between races more common than thought." *University of Michigan News and Information Service* (2000). www.umich.edu/~newsinfo/Releases/2000/Mar00/r032300a.html (accessed 11/26/01).

5   "The Army Has Virtually Put an End to Jim Crow: Is There a Lesson Here for Higher Education?" *Journal of Blacks in Higher Education* (JBHE), Number 13, Autumn 1996, p. 135.

6   "The Equal Opportunity Army." *The Globalist*, August 31, 2001. www.theglobalist.com/nor/richter/2001/08-31-01.stml (accessed 1/28/02).

7   Ibid.

8   www.multiracial.com.

9   www.poppolitics.com/articles/2000-06-19-crossing.shtml.

10   Wright, Marguerite A. *I'm Chocolate, You're Vanilla: Raising Healthy Black and Biracial Children in a Race-Conscious World*. San Francisco, CA: Jossey-Bass, 1998.

Chapter 5: Your People

1   Burnette, Erin. "The Strengths of Mixed-Race Relationships." *American Psychological Association's Monitor on Psychology*. September 1995.

2   *Washington Post*, Henry J. Kaiser Family Foundation, and Harvard University (2001) Race, Dating, and Marriage Poll. *Washington Post* (July 5, 2001).

3   Glazer, Nathan. *We Are All Multiculturalists Now*. Cambridge, MA: Harvard University Press, 1997.

Chapter 7: Local and Regional Flavor

1   *New York Times* staff. "How Race Is Lived in America." *New York Times* (July 2000). www.nytimes.com/learning/general/specials/race/index.html (accessed 11/26/01).

2   Sack, K., and Elder, J. "Poll Finds Optimistic Outlook but Enduring Racial Division." *New York Times* (July 13, 2000). http://www.nytimes.com/learning/general/featured_articles/000713thursday.html (accessed 11/27/01).

3 Clark, William, author of *The California Cauldron* (Guilford Press, 1998) and professor of geography at UCLA.

4 Pollard, K. M., and O'Hare, W. P. *America's Racial and Ethnic Minorities.* Washington, DC: Population Reference Bureau, 1999. www.prb.org/Template.cfm?Section=PRB&template=/ContentManagement/ContentDisplay.cfm&ContentID=3471 (accessed 11/26/01).

5 Tatum, Beverly Daniel. *Why Are All the Black Kids Sitting Together in the Cafeteria?* New York: Basic Books, 1997.

6 Bohmer, D. "Why Are All the Black Kids Sitting Together in the Cafeteria?" *Family Education* (2001). www.familyeducation.com/article/0,1120,1-3482,00.html (accessed 11/26/01).

7 The SPLC defines *active* as having engaged in "criminal acts, marches, rallies, speeches, meetings, leafleting or publishing." A *hate group* is defined as any organization having "beliefs or practices that attack or denigrate an entire class of people, typically for their beliefs or immutable characteristics."

8 Friedman, Robert. *Upstart Small Business Legal Guide.* Chicago: Dearborn Financial Publishing, Inc., 1998.

Chapter 8: "Best" Places to Live

1 All population and racial breakdowns of such come from the U.S. Census Bureau's 2000 census statistics.

2 Information on active hate groups was found at the Southern Poverty Law Center's Intelligence Project Web site: http://splcenter.org/intelligenceproject/ip-index.html.

3 Information on local hate crimes comes from the FBI's Uniform Crime reports and reflects crimes reported in 2000 (except where noted) where the reporting agency has defined race as the "bias motivation." The FBI reports annually on hate crimes, and the most recent statistics can be found at their Web site: www.fbi.gov/ucr/ucr.htm.

4 http://groups.yahoo.com/group/racerelationsaustintexas.

5 For information, contact dlk@mail.utexas.edu.

6 Average rental prices are based on reports from the Homestore.com rent calculator. www.springstreet.com/apartments/fyp/rentcalc/rent_calc.jhtml.

7 www.ameasite.org/bfn.asp.

8 See the Resources section for contact information.

9 As reported by Howard County police in 2000.

10 http://columbiamaryland.com/colum1a.htm.

11 www.sunspot.net/news/local/howard/bal-columbia-part3.story.

12 www.primenet.com/~dsmyre/mac.htm.

13 The director of this program is Barb Jones, and she may be contacted at 4100 28th Avenue South, Minneapolis, MN 55406, (612) 729-7397.

14 To contact West Point Assembly International, call (612) 721-8788. Worship is Sunday mornings at the Riverview Theatre, 10 A.M.

15 www.njgift.org.

16 www.swirlinc.org.

17 For information, contact: LEdwards4C@aol.com.

18 www.multiracialjewishnet.org.

19 For information, contact: david_seibel@ml.com.

20 See the Resources section for contact information.

21 www.oregonlive.com/special/census/index.ssf?/news/oregonian/01/03/lc_31divrs27.
frame.

22 www.isomedia.com/homes/Duncan/interracial.html.

23 www.mavin.org.

24 http://archives.seattletimes.nwsource.com/cgi-bin/texis/web/vortex/display?slug=race
&date=19960505.

25 All cost-of-living estimations are based on the ACCRA Cost of Living Index where 100
is the national average.

26 Call Lynn Coriano at (206) 389-7337, send e-mail to lynnc@seattlechamber.com, or
visit www2.seattlechamber.com/uec/initiatives/racc.htm.

Chapter 9: Interracial Relationships Abroad

1 Monroy, E. "Left-Wing Anti-Miscegenation." *Interracial Voice*. www.webcom.com/
~intvoice/emily2.html (accessed 11/29/01).

2 "Something Old, Something New." *Sydney Morning Herald*, October 11, 2000. old.
smh.com.au/news/0010/11/text/features1.html (accessed 11/27/01).

3 Britain's Commission for Racial Equality: www.cre.gov.uk.

4 To join, visit www.liveabroad.com/index.html.

5 See www.transitionsabroad.com for subscription information.

6 www.escapeartist.com.

Chapter 10: Planning an Interracial Wedding

1 www.askginka.com.

2 www.weddingzone.net/px-tr003.htm.

3 www.ultimatewedding.com/articles/get.php?action=getarticle&articleid=307.

4 www.theknot.com.

5 www.theknot.com/ch_article.html?Object=A00127110357&keyword=Religion%20%
26%20Rituals&channel=planning&subchannel=Religion%20%26%20Rituals.

Chapter 11: Under the Magnifying Glass

1 www.pub.umich.edu/daily/1997/oct/10-06-97/news/news3.html.

2 A copy of this paper may be purchased for four dollars from the Publications Department, Wellesley Centers for Women, Wellesley College, 106 Central Street, Wellesley, MA
02481. Make checks payable to the Wellesley Centers for Women.

3 http://bcn.boulder.co.us/campuspress/2000/11/16/dating20001116.html.

4 Burnette, Erin. "The Strengths of Mixed-Race Relationships." *American Psychological Association's Monitor on Psychology*. September 1995.

Chapter 12: Handling Discrimination

1 Morin, R., and Cottman, M. H. "Discrimination's Lingering Sting." *Washington Post*, Friday, June 22, 2001. www.washingtonpost.com/wp-dyn/articles/A29002-2001Jun21.html (accessed 3/28/02).

2 Ibid.

3 Ibid.

4 PBS's *An American Love Story* Web site is www.pbs.org/weblab/lovestories.

5 "An American Love Story: The Ups and Downs of an Interracial Family." *Dialogues Online: Racial Healing in Our Communities*. www.digitalcity.com/honolulu/dialogue/main.adp?page=americanfamily (accessed 5/15/02).

Chapter 13: Raising Biracial Kids

1 www.mavinfoundation.org.

2 Two good resources for managing children's hair are Collison, Michele N-K, *It's All Good Hair: The Guide to Styling and Grooming Black Children's Hair*, New York: Amistad Press, 2002; and Ferrell, Pamela, *Kids Talk Hair: An Instruction Book for Grown-Ups & Kids*, Washington, DC: Cornrows and Co., 1999.

Chapter 14: Medical Matters

1 Lewis, R. "Genetic Screening Fetal Signs on a Journey of Discovery." FDA Consumer Magazine. December 1990. www.fda.gov/bbs/topics/consumer/con00025.html (accessed 7/3/02).

2 Entine, J., and Satel, S. "Race Belongs in the Stem Cell Debate." *Washington Post*, September 9, 2001, page B01. www.washingtonpost.com/wp-dyn/articles/A60970-2001Sep8.html.

3 Ibid.

4 "You can't use a child's own cord blood to cure him. If he had a genetic condition, you'd be giving him back his old disorder. If he had cancer, you'd be giving him the same immune system that failed to defeat the cancer in the first place."

Chapter 15: Giving Them the Best of Both Worlds

1 "Helping Children Develop a Sense of Identity." Scholastic.com. http://teacher.scholastic.com/professional/teachdive/identity.htm (accessed 2/05/02).

2 Freedman, Judy S. *Easing the Teasing*. New York: Contemporary Books, 2002.

3 Freedman, Judy. "Easing the Teasing Strategies." www.easingtheteasing.com/proto4.html (accessed 5/17/02).

4 "Dealing with Bullies." KidsHealth.org. http://kidshealth.org/kid/feeling/emotion/bullies.html (accessed 2/05/02).